Daughters
and their Dads

A book for

- fathers
- adult daughters
- husbands
- father-figures

Bruce Robinson

MACSIS
PUBLISHING
PERTH

This book is dedicated to three of the fathers and one of the children whom I interviewed for a previous book, *Fathering from the Fast Lane*, all of whom have since died unexpectedly - Tim Willoughby, Brian Edwards, Harry Perkins and Daniel McCluskey.

Their lives inspired me and their untimely deaths remind me of how important it is for every man to think about how to be a good dad and father-figure whilst you still have the chance, because you don't have forever.

Bruce Robinson

Daughters and their Dads :
This edition first published in 2008 in Australia by MACSIS Publishing, ABN 71 264 006 446, Perth, WA 6008, Australia. www.macsis.com.au

Text design and graphics by Geoff & Kerry De Filippis
Cover photographs and design by Scott Robinson and Kerry De Filippis
Illustrations by Chris Morgan
Edited by Cailey Raffel & Amy Robinson
Printed by Lamb Printing, East Perth
Book website: www.brucerobinson.com.au/daughters

Photo credits The author wishes to acknowledge the following for their kind contribution of photographs: Francis Andrijich (Beazley), Bill Bachman (Winton), Broderick Photography (Rudd), the Office of the Prime Minister (Howard), Brendan Read and The Australian Women's Weekly (Anderson), West Australian Newspapers Ltd (Cometti, Edwards), Allsports (G.Marsh, Gould, R.Marsh), The Age (Nossal), BBC and National Library of Australia (Lillee).

Contents

Preface

It is easy to be motivated to write about daughters and their dads but it is hard to know exactly how to write such a book. It is such an important issue that I want the book to be read by men and women. No one style will suit all, so this book has several styles in the hope that every reader will be able to access some helpful ideas to try.

Assumptions

In writing this book I am assuming that:

- fathers and mothers want the best for their daughters and are open to new ideas
- adult daughters want to understand how their relationship with their father might be affecting their adult relationships, especially with males
- women also want to grow from any hurt they have felt from their father and not be disabled by it
- husbands want the best for their wives
- most men who have influence over young girls (e.g. grandfathers, schoolteachers) want to help them reach their full potential and live lives of contentment and fulfilment.

What is different about this book?

This book differs from other father-daughter books because:

1. It targets not just fathers but *adult* daughters who are impacted by their fathers, *husbands* who are also impacted by their wife's relationship with her father and, importantly, *father-figures* such as grandfathers and schoolteachers, who can have a profound impact on a girl's life.

2. It combines published research with many personal stories, with road-tested suggestions that are drawn from the real lives of many different people.

3. Rather than describing problems it focuses on solutions and provides *realistic strategies, tips and ideas.*

The use of published information in this book

To research this issue of dads and daughters I have read over 2000 published articles from a variety of sources. I have also read over 40 published books of relevance to this subject as well as newspaper interviews, websites and published interviews.

What is clear is that there is not a lot of quality publications discussing this issue, despite its importance.[1,2] Some of the more 'measurable' issues are well studied (e.g. sex, pregnancy, drugs, alcohol and divorce) but the ones that are harder to measure are not (e.g. unconditional love and specialness).

This need for more quality research about fathers and daughters has been identified by others.[3-9]

Such research is difficult to do because of the complexities involved[10-12] and the need for well-executed qualitative studies,[13] which are hard to undertake.

I have tried to quote studies which I think are not biased, use sufficient numbers to draw valid conclusions, are peer reviewed (at least as much as possible in this field), represent a consensus or majority view and which take into account confounding issues such as poverty, race and culture. I have not tried to quote every valid study on each subject, just those that make the relevant point.

The use of personal interview quotes in this book

I initially asked people about their personal stories because my own experience and the published literature on the subject were so limited. But the more people I interviewed the more I realised that personal quotes and stories provide more diverse information than published studies. My sample of interviewees is broad but not random, so their comments are not presented as a scientific study but as a rich mine of ideas and strategies that have worked for others.

Men and women learn more from listening to useful ideas and personal stories than from a lot of statistics, generalisations and lecturing about parenting. Stories are a good way to communicate about daughters and their dads so the information and ideas I received from the interviews provide most of the best ideas in this book.

Importantly, in all but a few cases, the interviewees have allowed me to put their name to these quotes. Sometimes (e.g. when discussing abuse) they requested that their quotes stay in the book but that the name be altered to protect their identity but still allow the reader to follow their specific quotes in the book. However this is not common. Occasionally I have used a quote which was not obtained during a personal interview of the subject by me, in which case the source of that quote is clearly referenced.

The feedback I have received from many people is that reading other people's stories is very helpful. The willingness of so many different types of fathers and daughters from different social situations, with good or poor relationships, to share their ideas has already been helpful to many.

Who was interviewed?

My interviewees come from 15 different countries, though most come in roughly equal proportions from Australia, United Kingdom and North America, the three areas in which I have lived for long periods of time.

Those interviewed include actors, artists, authors, baronesses, bikers, bodyguards, businessmen, carpenters, chaplains, convicts, directors, doctors, drug addicts, factory workers, farmers, floor sanders, football team owners, hairdressers, housewives, househusbands, journalists, lawyers, media personalities, missionaries, mountaineers, musicians, Nobel Prize winners, nurses, occupational therapists, Olympic gold medallists, nurses, parenting experts, pastors, pig farmers, pilots, plumbers policemen, politicians, prostitutes, psychologists, refugees, reporters, rock band managers, sailors, schoolteachers, screenwriters, soldiers, sole-parent mothers, spitfire pilots, sports stars, stonemasons, students, taxi drivers, Test cricketers, TV presenters, typists, underground miners, vignerons and others.

There are as many 'ordinary people' as there are high profile interviewees. I interviewed many daughters, not just the fathers of daughters. The quotes listed thus reflect a wide range of views.

The 400 interviews lasted 60,000 minutes and produced about one million quotable words. This represents about 17,200 years of experience of being a father, father-figure or a daughter – a valuable source of ideas. This makes the book unique and has generated many insights that you won't have read anywhere else.

Names, occupations and locations are provided for all interviewees, except of course those few who requested that we modify their names for the sake of anonymity.

Rather than continually say 'former, past, current' etc, it was easier to use a single tense.

Why using these quotes is so powerful

The main advantages of using quotes and stories to convey messages about daughters and their dads are:

- the tips have been *'road-tested'*, i.e. they have worked or failed, not just been imagined
- they are *personal* stories rather than theoretical
- they are *authentic,* first hand stories, not second hand
- they represent people in *normal family life,* not just from counselling sessions
- they are from *varied* individuals from different countries and occupations
- they provide a range of *ideas* – you can't think of everything yourself
- they encourage dads to *break stereotypes,* e.g. tough sportsmen who hug their daughters
- they have the *benefit of hindsight* – how the issues of men and women eventually resolved
- they thus *encourage* men and women that things can work out despite awful circumstances
- they are all *interesting* people and fun to read

Many suggestions and ideas are listed. To be certain that the suggestions in the book are consistent with the views of key professional groups, I have had all of the quotes and ideas in the book reviewed by several professionals who deal with father–daughter issues; 5 psychologists, 3 social workers, 4 teachers, 4 pastors plus a group of other individuals (listed under Acknowledgements).

Why it's useful having a scientist-physician write this book

There are a number of reasons why my professional roles make me well suited to the task of writing this book.

As a *scientist* I am prone to asking 'why is this so?' and inevitably I do that whenever I see dysfunctional father-child relationships or their consequences. Also, as a scientist I am used to analysing published information to assess its validity in a critical, non-biased way. This is essential when discussing family issues because of the variable quality and biases of publications on these issues.

As a *physician* I talk with dying men who tell me how they wished they had lived their lives as better dads and women who wish their childhood had been happier. Their lack of access to helpful advice is what motivates me. Because I am also comfortable talking with people in distress and discussing their lives openly with them, interviewees trust me with the information I obtain and don't tend to be evasive or defensive. Indeed I found that personal interview technique was the best way to obtain new ideas rather than, for example, the written submissions I received.

Being a non-psychologist, family therapist or social scientist brings an independent perspective to the topic – my focus is not primarily from the perspective of psychological disturbance.

Use of the words 'marriage', 'husbands' etc in this book

Mothers and fathers could be married, single, in de facto relationships or a number of other situations. For simplicity when I talk about stable male-female relationships in this book I use the words 'marriage', 'husband' and 'wife' for convenience. I acknowledge however that there are other parenting arrangements for which this book is applicable. No offence is meant by just using just the words 'marriage', 'husband' and 'wife'.

Possible ways to read this book

It might seem silly to make suggestions to a reader about how to read a book like this. But I will make some because others have found such suggestions very useful.

 You suggested that the men read chapters of this book together over breakfast or coffee. They responded to that and it has made a big difference to them all.

Diedre Ranford – homemaker, Como

It would be difficult to read the material in this book at one continuous sitting. Perhaps you might consider reading a section then thinking about it for a while and talking about it with someone.

It is easy to feel swamped, even exhausted, by lists so perhaps just *pick only one idea at a time* from each list to try.

You might wish to consider reading this book with a pen in your hand in order to mark the specific ideas that you wish to try.

The ideas presented are not instructional. It may be helpful to see this book as a 'supermarket of ideas' rather than a 'schoolbook'. That means readers can pick those ideas that suit them and leave the rest. Also, it means that at a later time they might choose some other ideas from the book to try. Others will pick different ideas 'off the shelf' based on personality and circumstances.

You might also consider *reading it with your daughter,* or your father if you are female, and discussing it together.

Many men and women have told me that they find it most effective to approach this sort of book by *forming a small discussion group* to read and talk about each chapter over breakfast or coffee, weekly or monthly.

You might find it useful to give the book to someone to read, e.g. your father, wife, husband or father-figure, asking them to read a particular section which you think might be relevant to them.

It is easy to feel inadequate or guilty when reading about all the good things other parents do. I often felt like that after my interviews but I resolved to try just one new thing from what I had learnt during each interview. It helped me to not feel so swamped.

Others have realised that many of these tips are useful for mothers as well as for fathers, and for sons as well as daughters.

> *This book is terrific and it has made me think a lot about how I treat and relate to my daughter and wife....and my son for that matter.*

Jim Watterston – Director, Department of Education and Early Childhood Development, Melbourne

Because the book is limited by size, I have included additional material for each chapter plus all the references on the book's website: www.brucerobinson.com.au/daughters

My dream is that every girl will have a father or father-figure in her life who believes in her, loves her without condition, spends time with her, sees her beauty, listens to her and helps her develop into a confident, loving, thoughtful, successful person capable of kindness and intimacy.

Acknowledgements

I acknowledge the two most important women in my life – my wife Jacqueline and my daughter Amy. They have humoured and tolerated me with enormous patience as I learnt, slowly and often reluctantly, the importance of the issues discussed in this book.

I am also extremely grateful to the 400 interviewees for making the time available to talk with me, often more than once, for being honest with me and for taking the time to check the text and provide me with photos.

I also wish to thank the following for their invaluable help getting this manuscript completed: Geoff and Kerry De Filippis, Cailey Raffel and Amy, Jacqueline and Scott Robinson.

I also acknowledge the individuals who reviewed various parts of this book, including:

- *Teachers*
  Peter Prout
  Belinda Hotchkin
  Jim Watterston
  Sandy Robinson

- *Psychologists*
  Jenny Wright
  Jane Spry
  Phyllis Prout
  Eve Bowtell
  Christabel Chamarette

- *Pastors*
  Kanishka Raffel
  Ian Robinson
  Peter Prout
  Warwick Marsh

- *Social Workers and Counsellors*
  Yvonne de Blanc
  Noel Giblett
  Pauline Dixon
  Sarah Mumford

- *Others*
  including Amy Robinson, Michael Hotchkin,
  Jacqueline Robinson and Susan Maushart.

Rex Finch and Sean Doyle also made helpful suggestions.

The comments and suggestions of all of these individuals are highly valued. I take full responsibility for the final text and do not wish to imply that everything said in the text represents the professional opinions of all of the above individuals.

 There was something about my dad's love for me that was more a choice than being automatic.

But I knew that because my dad loved me I was worth loving.

I have certainly come across people in my working life where they were not affirmed by their father and it has had a big negative influence on them.

Rosemary Kendell – occupational therapist, Floreat

Chapter 1

The importance of the father-daughter relationship

"Dads have a profound effect on their daughters - for good or bad"

CHAPTER TOPICS

- Why fathers are important in a daughter's life
- What daughters really need from their dads
- Mothers and the role of fathering

Why the father-daughter relationship is important

There is an incredible power in the father-daughter relationship, a power which strongly influences a woman's future, for good or bad. Girls long for affection and affirmation from their fathers. The influence that fathers have on their daughters is profound and lasts for the whole of their lives and it creates a hole in their lives if it is absent.[1-6]

> Fathers and daughters need each other. A dad can give a daughter a special confidence and sense of her own value in a very special way. A strong father/daughter bond helps a daughter navigate through the many tough challenges of the teenage years and early adulthood.

Kevin Rudd – Prime Minister of Australia, Canberra

Many published studies have confirmed the powerful effect that fathers have on daughters, with few dissenting voices.[7-17]

The fact that women are profoundly influenced by a father and/or by father-figures worries me for two reasons.

Firstly, I have a daughter whom I love. When I look at my daughter and I think about how much she is being shaped by her relationship with me, I get a bit nervous – am I doing a good job of that? Am I doing the right things? How do I know what she really needs from me compared with her two brothers and how do I know how well I am doing?

As adults, women often think about their dads -

how things were and how they wish they had been

Secondly, I have a wife whom I also love, and I have found out that the way a woman relates to men is profoundly influenced by the relationship she had with her own father. I confess that I was slow to realise that, like a lot of husbands. So when I look at my wife now I think about how much she was inevitably affected by her relationship with her own father and I wonder whether I really understand that, whether I've shown enough interest in the issue and been willing to discuss it with her.

As adults, women often think about their dads - how things were and how they wish they had been. Most of the other women I spoke to have also sought to understand their relationship with their father. My wife has too and I have learnt from that.

Many dads tell me how slow they have been to appreciate the power of the father-daughter relationship in their family. That slowness is common and is described in the literature.[18,19] Interestingly, by the time girls reach adolescence they are more aware of how important their dads are to them than the dads are themselves.[20]

Hopefully as you read this book you will understand that relationship better yourself.

> I talk to young women training to be teachers who say how much they were influenced - good and bad - by their dads. Unfortunately the negative side seems to be a constant longing by young women for their dad's approval; is that why they fall into relationships with men where they are looking for a father's approval, rather than a relationship of equals? I suspect so.

Peter Prout – farmer, soldier, lecturer in Education, teacher, pastor, Subiaco

The special needs of daughters versus sons

Hardly any of the men that I ask can tell me what it is that their daughters need from them, as distinct from their sons.

A respected family psychologist in Colorado Springs, Dr James Dobson, told me recently that a major factor that determines whether or not a woman is likely to have a successful long term relationship with a man is the relationship that she had with her father.[18] This is also true with regards to the confidence that a woman brings to her life. It is not the only factor and there are many other things that affect these outcomes of course. A number of studies support this notion.[21-23]

There is something particular in the relationship between daughters and their fathers that represents a powerful bond, a powerful potential influence, for good or bad. Sometimes dads tell me that all kids need one thing - love. I used to think that too. Just love them all and have good times with them and teach them stuff and everything would be OK. This is not so.

The father-daughter relationship is powerful in shaping a woman's future - but most fathers are not aware of this

Dads need to be aware that there are several ways a daughter's future is peculiarly influenced by the relationship with her father. It is incorrect to say that girls only need the same inputs as boys - this is true to a point, but there are some things that are particularly important for girls.

All of my interviews and reading have taught me that a daughter has special needs from her father, especially:

- approval of her *attractiveness* as a person, her beauty, including acceptance of her body shape [24]

- encouragement to make her *confident* to function in this world, including the confidence to say 'no' to drugs and to think and learn for herself [25]

- understanding what she should expect in her *relationships with men*, including a healthy view of sexuality [26]

Also, I discovered in my interviews and in the published literature that there are special ways in which the fundamental needs of all children are slightly different when applied to a daughter, especially they way we show

- that we love her *unconditionally* [27]
- that we are willing to *listen* to her [28]
- that we understand and reinforce how *special* she is as a person, including doing one-on-one activities with her. [29]

These inputs help to determine how kind a woman is to herself, how free she feels to be kind to others or whether she dislikes herself, even becoming self-destructive.

It was when I found this out that I first became really concerned about my own performance as a father. Once I realised that as Amy's father my role was important and not optional, that I have a profound effect on her life for good or bad, I asked myself how well I was doing. Was I behaving in a way that will help her in her important relationships, not hinder them? And was I giving her confidence in herself rather than eroding that confidence?

I had, up until then, thought I had been doing a pretty good job as a dad. But then I realised there were many things I just wasn't doing because I wasn't aware that my daughter needed anything different from what my sons needed.

The strategies listed in this book can strengthen the bond between a father and his daughter and help equip a daughter for life. What that means in reality won't be the same for every child, because every child is unique. And it won't be the same for every dad, because every dad is different. Also, not all dads reading this will be living in the same house as their children. Not every idea, tip and strategy will suit every reader so just take and use those that you find helpful. This is not an instruction manual but a collection of ideas that will suit different people at different times.

Why <u>fathers of daughters</u> should read this book

This book is partly written for fathers of daughters, because it will give them insight and strategies that will help them provide for the real needs of their daughters. Hopefully this information will help dads to make changes whilst their daughters are still young and able to benefit. I am grateful myself that I learnt so much from these interviews and ideas whilst my daughter was young. But these are ideas that will help a father at any age or stage - it is never too late to work on the father-daughter relationship, and there are many examples of that in this book.

> It is never too late to work on the father-daughter relationship

When dad is present in a girl's life she receives strong signals from him that affect her life, often profoundly, and he must understand how important those signals are.

> When you teach her, she learns more rapidly. When you guide her, she gains confidence. If you fully understood just how profoundly you can influence your daughter's life, you would be terrified, overwhelmed, or both.
>
> Many fathers (particularly of teen girls) think their daughters need to figure out life on their own.
>
> But your daughter faces a world markedly different from the one you did growing up: it's less friendly, morally unmoored, and even outright dangerous.

Meg Meeker – adolescent health physician[30]

Knowing what to do as a father of sons is hard enough, but doing a good job of being a father to daughters is not intuitive for men – we have never been girls. A book like this helps fill those gaps in our knowledge before it is too late to realise we don't know what we are doing.

Over recent years there has been an attempt by many fathers to spend more time with their kids.[31] But as lives get busier this is harder to achieve. For example, although most fathers say that the evening family meal is important, less than half of them succeed in attending it most nights.[32] Also, many dads tell me they just don't know *how* to talk with their kids when they do spend time with them.

The need to think about fathering and to change what we do was illustrated to me by what one man said to me after reading *Fathering from the Fast Lane*. This man is a tough welder and when we talked about his own children, what he said surprised me.

> I read a little bit of the book and I have to stop because I am crying so much. It reminds me of what I should have done with my kids. My kids were 'just there' and I thought that was enough for them. I never realised how much they really wanted me to do things with them until many years later. I will be a better grandfather for it all, but it is too late for my own kids as they have all left home now. I wish I'd known all of this stuff when I started my fathering.

Peter Provan – welder, Quinn's Rocks

Most men are not aware of the power of a father-daughter relationship

Given that few men can identify what it is that their daughters need from them as distinct from their sons, we need to focus on that issue.

Dads lack basic knowledge about being a girl - they have never been girls themselves and their father never taught them how to be a good dad to a daughter. Often they have never read or heard anything on the subject. Indeed there is not much written on the subject of fathers and daughters, nor much spoken about in the media.

Another problem is that of male discomfort with girly things – men often feel more comfortable doing things with sons rather than with daughters. Certainly boys need a father-figure in their life but dads need to not let their desire to help their sons keep them from engaging with their daughters.

A hairdresser told me one day the following moving story about her father, a story which illustrates the block that some dads have thinking about what their daughters need from them:

My dad was a really good father - to my brother. They were very close and did lots of things together and are still very close even to this day.

For example every morning at 5 o'clock my dad would come in and knock on my brother's bedroom door and together the two of them would go off to train our family racehorse. But he never made any effort to do things with me.

Once a month now I get together with Dad for lunch. But after two minutes we run out of things to say to each other because he never really formed any sort of close relationship with me. If he had bothered to do that, I would have really looked forward to those lunches. But he never did. But, you know, each morning at 5 o'clock as Dad came to get my brother to go and train our horse, I bet that he thought I was asleep in my bedroom. But I wasn't.

Each morning I would be lying there, waiting and listening and hoping that once, just once, he would knock on my door instead.

Shelley Grove – hairdresser, Sydney

What I find scary is that this is not a story of a girl growing up in a terrible family. There is no alcoholism or abuse to blame. It is about a good dad who just didn't realise how important he was to his daughter and a daughter who was too shy to demand his attention or didn't feel she could.

Separated dads

Virtually every suggestion in the book applies to dads who do not live in the same house as their children. There are some specific suggestions made for separated dads in Chapter 12. In general the needs of girls are much the same wherever the father lives, though the living circumstances and contact arrangements will necessitate additional attention.

Why <u>adult daughters</u> should read this book

Adult daughters could read this book for 3 reasons:

- as a *daughter* to try to better understand her reactions to events in her life, especially in her marriage
- as a *co-parent*, to encourage their husband to be a better father
- as a *mother* who is considering finding good father-figures for her daughter

Understanding issues relating to your own father

One reason why adult daughters might read a book like this is to help understand more about who she is and why she is the way she is. Given that most women are powerfully influenced by their father or other strong father-figures in their lives, it would be surprising if women could not learn a lot about themselves by reading about what a girl really needs from a father. It will probably become obvious to her, as she reads, whether she did or did not receive those things.

And because there are many areas in which the father-daughter influence can be manifest in an adult woman's life, it is not surprising that women begin to think about such issues if they experience a lack of confidence in life, feelings of unattractiveness, low self-esteem, extreme mood swings, anxiety, difficulties in relationships with a partner, problems with sexual intimacy or controlling behaviour.[33-35]

Many women, as they get older, begin to develop insight into how their relationship with their father might have affected them. Indeed many women then seek to understand that relationship with their father, or lack of relationship, and try to understand themselves and their own reactions to their friends, partner, children and work colleagues. It is often in marriage that they begin to see these issues as being important.

When our marriage hit a difficult patch I realised that there were things that I hadn't resolved from my childhood that were interfering with our relationship.

Brenda Hodges – teacher, Sydney

Thus it is important for women to read this book to help them understand their own experience of their dads and other father-figures, their marriage and their own children. For some women, such memories and insights may be triggered by this book.

The importance of each of the issues raised in this book to individual women will vary – I have noticed that the significance of these things is often only apparent to women later in life. A whole chapter is devoted to resolution, forgiveness and reconciliation between daughters and fathers (Chapter 13). I hope that women will hand this book around to each other and discuss together how each issue might have affected them.

Why aren't mothers enough?

Sometimes I am asked by mothers, 'Why are fathers so important - aren't mothers enough?' This is a tough question to handle, especially when talking to sole-parent mums. There is often so much emotion in that question that I think of looking for a way out of answering it. But I can't and I don't, because the question is too important.

All the research and all my interviews point convincingly to the same conclusion - girls do much better in life with a father involved[6-17] or, if he is not around, or not helpful, a strong father-figure.[36-39]

Many families with one parent do well. Single mothers do amazing work in difficult circumstances, succeeding at a job far harder than most of us can possibly imagine. They deserve our respect and they deserve our support. And millions of children have strong, loving relationships with their non-resident dads. But on the whole, we must never forget children need their dads, and when they're absent, something is lost.

George Bush – US President,
Washington DC [40]

Mothers have a role in possibly helping their children's father be a better dad. Many dads that I have spoken to have told me that they really only learnt how to parent by asking or watching their wives.

Another reason why mothers might read this book in their role as co-parents with the father is that they are well placed to 'interpret' a father's words and behaviour for the children in a positive way, if appropriate.

 It was my mother who translated Dad's love for us into words – she would explain to me how much my father loved me even though he had difficulty expressing it. That was important for me.

Christine Jenkins – physician, Sydney

Mothers are often the 'gatekeepers' of a child's access to good fathering, whether he lives in another location or in some families, even if he lives in the family home.[41,42] This can be a positive or negative role.

Perhaps if you are a mother reading this book you might consider inviting your daughter's father to read it. This is important, even if your relationship with your daughter's father is poor. You might also encourage your child's school to have father-friendly strategies.

You need to target mothers, because if they don't understand how important fathers are to children it is very hard to achieve anything.

Jim Watterston – Director, Department of Education and Early Childhood Development, Melbourne

Mothers as co-parents with fathers

At the very beginning I am keen to emphasise that this book in no way devalues the role of mothers in the lives of their daughters. On the contrary, it is impossible to over emphasise the importance of the relationship between mothers and daughters and the powerful role that women play in children's lives. There is also no doubt that some adult daughters have ongoing relationship difficulties with their mothers rather than their fathers.[43] But this book only focusses on fathers.

It is worth mentioning here that most of the tips in this book are just as relevant to mothers as to fathers. Girls need to hear most of these messages from their mothers too. But I have focussed on fathers because of their great need and because, as a man, I did not wish to tell mothers what to do.

Good fathering allows mothers to get on with doing a good job of mothering

Mothers tend to do a good job of mothering, and to think about that role, whether they are married or single, at home or working, healthy or prone to illness. Not always, but usually. But it is hard to be the mother you want to be when you are doing all the parenting – better fathering allows mothers to get on with doing a good job of mothering.

For example, one of the reasons that kids do better at school if a caring father is involved is because it allows mothers to now give children the personal and educational attention they need from them, rather than being busy and distracted doing all of the parenting. Indeed a 2006 study of 237 families showed that having a supportive mother and father was clearly associated with higher scores in mental functioning compared to having either parent alone.[44]

And many fathers already do a great job too. But it is common that fathers are not pulling their weight when it comes to parenting, leaving a lot of it to mothers. When that happens the children and the fathers miss out. Because fathers often worry less than mothers about their own performance as parents, they rarely read books or attend seminars on the subject.

Another good reason to have fathers more involved as co-parents is that mothers are human and thus are not always in good shape. When fathers are present in a child's life, whether in the same house or not, they provide support when mothers go through difficult periods (e.g. times of stress or depression) and vice versa, and this has been shown to be an important safeguard in a child's life.[45]

> Most husbands, and some wives, aren't aware of how much their marriage is influenced by the relationship she had with her father

It is important that all mothers, as co-parents with their child's father, read a book like this and be aware of the importance of the relationship between their daughter and her father so that she encourages that relationship out of love for her daughter. If a mother doesn't encourage that relationship, it may not happen.

Why <u>husbands</u> should read this book

Most husbands, and some wives, aren't aware of how much their marital relationship is influenced by the relationship the wife had with her father. If that relationship was strong and rich, this may not matter too much, but when it has negative components it becomes important to understand them so that it doesn't interfere with the marriage. It has taken me a while to begin to understand that in my own life.

Men, have you ever sat there listening to your wife reacting to something and thought 'I wonder why she is so sensitive to this?' I have often done that and been perplexed. Or have you wondered why despite being competent, she lacks confidence or why despite being attractive she often feels unattractive? I have done that too. Have you wondered why she is so sensitive to criticism given in a certain way or why she reacts to particular issues?

I have noticed that many men get surprised by their wife's strong reactions to seemingly innocuous events. I do too. It is a caring and worthwhile thing to consider where those feelings might be coming from, though this can be tricky.

" I remember watching the Barbara Streisand film 'Yentl'. They had such a sweet relationship, that daughter with her father. I sat in the cinema and just started crying and couldn't stop.

It caught me by surprise and Bob was surprised too. I had missed out on that kind of relationship and it really struck me at that time. Fathers need to make their daughters feel precious to him.

Carol Hamrin – consultant on China, Virginia

Not all of a woman's surprising reactions will be able to be traced back to her relationship with her father. But you will realise, when you read this book, that it is a good place to start looking.

I didn't really understand how important that was in the first few years of our marriage (maybe the first 20 years of our marriage!) but I think I am seeing it more clearly now. I am a bit of a slow learner and should have seen it earlier. I used to fob it off and think my wife was overanalysing things. But as I have learnt more about my father-in-law and some of the hardships in his life and watched how he talks to my wife, I have realised how right she is. He is a wonderful man whom I love deeply, but he would never claim to have done his fathering perfectly. I wish I had had the insight to understand more of that when we were a young married couple.

By understanding what it is that a daughter needs from her father you will be better placed to talk to your partner about her relationship with her father. You might even go through this book with her, asking her to talk about each issue and her experience of that issue. And when you do that you will have a much clearer understanding of her. You might become less confused.

Try to understand your wife's issues with her father

Because the way a daughter is fathered has a profound effect on her subsequent relationships, particularly her marriage, husbands need to understand how their wife's relationship with her father is affecting her in adult life. We have discussed already how disabling those effects can be to communication, intimacy, confidence and sex in the relationship.

If we do not understand how our wife related to her father we risk getting confused and annoyed, for example when she reacts to what appears to be an innocent comment.

So husbands, try to understand so that you are not bewildered. When I talk to other husbands they have had the same experience in the early years of marriage they hardly ever thought of how their wife's relationship with her father might be impacting on their marriage. It was only after many years of marriage, lots of discussion, some arguments and sometime illness or the death of the father-in-law that they became aware of the effect of her relationship with her father, or lack of relationship, on their marriage.

> *For the first 5 years of our marriage I didn't think about Cailey's relationship with her father. That began to change when we had our first daughter. I learnt more about it in the period when her father was dying, but it is still something we haven't talked about much.*

Kanishka Raffel – lawyer, pastor, Shenton Park

Given that most divorces happen in those early years it seems wise to think about these things early. It wasn't for lack of input from my wife that I failed in those early years. It was because I didn't really listen. I discounted a lot of what she said because I didn't have the insight and willingness to really consider what she was saying.

Others have noted a similar slowness to understand these issues.

> *I have known for a long time that the father-daughter relationship is important, but interestingly I have only ever thought about that issue as a parent, not as a husband.*
>
> *This might be an important factor in helping to understand my wife's strong reactions to things.*

Michael Tarca – engineer, Claremont

I hope you will not be as slow as I was to see how father-daughter issues affect a marriage.

I don't mean to imply that understanding how your wife was influenced by her father makes a husband a passive observer of things. Although the marriage will be affected, the male partner is in a position to at least partially fill empty emotional spaces. Men, we could think about understanding those emotional spaces in the woman we love, e.g. by reading through this sort of book and thinking about the issues as they might affect her, and by talking with her about the issues.

Help and encourage her to think through them and don't get in the way of her doing so. She may need professional help to sort things out and it is vital that you are supportive during that time. Remember, if she is reacting to you because of how she related to her father, it is not you, not your marriage and not her love for you that is in question, even though it seems that way.

By understanding where a wife's reactions come from, husbands are in a position to deliberately not react the same way her father did, i.e. he can break the cycle. Also, understanding can change annoyance into empathy.

> By understanding what it is that a daughter needs from her father you will be better placed to talk to your partner about her relationship with her father

We could help by filling in some of those empty emotional spaces with words and deeds where possible. So, for example, if she was forgotten on her birthday, make a fuss of her every birthday; if she was never made to feel special, think of all the things that make her special and tell her; if she was never made to feel beautiful, tell her how beautiful she is, even if she doesn't seem to believe you at first; if she was not listened to start asking her opinion on things and doing some 'harpoon' listening (see chapter 9).

However husbands are not there to fix things, nor to be a wife's therapist, nor to try to be the father that she never had. We can't. It is enough just to understand, listen and empathise. That is a great gift we can give our wives.

The ideas presented in the book are not 'heavy' and not difficult. In fact they are easy, a bit like remembering our wedding anniversary or putting out the garbage – they are not hard to do but just have to be remembered. How much time does it take for a father or grandfather to tell a girl she is beautiful or gifted? About 20 seconds. They just need to think of doing it. That is why I want this book to be given to any father or father-figure because most won't think about saying these things, or know what to say, without those extra bits of help and encouragement to do so.

I also don't wish to induce 'over-parenting'. That sometimes occurs when people begin to understand what kids really need from them. But over-parenting, i.e. a life in which it is 'work + kids and nothing else' is a mistake because it puts too much pressure on kids (because they become a measure of a parent's success in life) and it doesn't role model for kids a life of rich friendships, community living and interesting child-free activities.

My aim in this book is not to make fathers feel even more guilty than they already do about their performance as fathers, but to give them greater understanding of the issues.

I also don't wish to disturb women as they consider their relationship with their fathers, if that consideration proves detrimental rather than helpful.

The book simply offers simple information plus a range of suggested strategies to improve the relationship that fathers have with daughters and that daughters have with their fathers and their husbands. It is also aimed at helping father-figures be strong, positive influences in a girl's life.

I encourage you to try them and discuss them.

Quiz Question

Who said: "I am a great writer because when I was a little girl and walked into a room where my father was sitting, his eyes would light up. There isn't any other reason."?

Answer: Toni Morrison – Nobel prize-winning novelist, b. 1931

The father-daughter relationship - some things to think about

Men

Understanding father-daughter relationships is important for all men.

We could read this book

- as *fathers*, to understand what we need to do as fathers of daughters

- as *husbands*, to understand our partners better

- as *father-figures*, asking ourselves how we can positively influence young girls

- as *community members*, to encourage other men such as brothers and friends to be good dads

Women

Understanding father-daughter relationships is also important for all women

- as *daughters*, to try to better understand their reactions to events in their lives, especially in marriage

- as *co-parents*, to help them encourage their partners to be better fathers

- as *community members*, to encourage other men such as brothers and friends to be good dads

- as *mothers* who need to find good father-figures for their daughters

> Fathers, sports coaches, teachers, any
> father-figure should seek to make kids feel
> special and give them confidence and belief
> in themselves.

Shane Gould – triple Olympic swimming gold medallist and
world record holder, Margaret River

Chapter 2

The powerful role of father-figures

"All girls can benefit from a good father-figure"

CHAPTER TOPICS

- Why father-figures are important for all girls
- Father-figures within the family
- Community father-figures

Why 'father-figures' are important

Any man who is a grandfather, stepfather, uncle, older brother, father-in-law, schoolteacher, youth leader, sports coach, pastor or family friend who has significant relationships with young girls is in a powerful position to influence them, positively or negatively.

Children with an active father-figure are at less risk of psychological and behaviour problems.[1-5] So I am talking about this early in this book in order that all potential father-figures, not just dads, think about the ideas presented.

Father-figures matter where dad is still around but they are especially important where there is no dad. Where dad is still around but not interested, or is even a negative influence on a daughter, then a father-figure can become a vital confidant, confidence builder and affirming influence.

> Most of the tips in this book relate to father-figures as much as to fathers

If there is no biological father around then I try to encourage sole-parent mothers to seek out appropriate father-figures. There is something definably unique that father-figures bring to a girl's life.[6] Although most women seek active father-figures for their children,[7] such a suggestion can meet with resistance if the mother has been badly hurt by men.

> I was abused as a child, and my two daughters have already been abused as children.
>
> I have a complete lack of trust in men and I've decided that I am going to be the one who is there for them – I will be their father and their mother all at one time. I don't trust men.

Nola Hooper – sole parent, Denver

At the outset I need to remind father-figures to be sensitive to what is appropriate and what is not appropriate in your relationship with a girl. This applies to what you say, how you say it, when and where you talk to her and how you behave towards her. A sensitivity to these things places you in a strong position be a trusted, safe alternative parent and a powerful voice in her life.

Many men are or can be father-figures. In reality a father-figure is any man who has significant contact with girls or young women. This contact could be as seemingly trivial as being the school bus driver. That role as a father-figure could be minimal, destructive or extraordinarily helpful to a young woman.

Some examples of potential father-figures
- grandfathers
- uncles
- school teachers
- coaches (sports, music)
- pastors/priests
- parent's of her friends
- neighbours
- school bus drivers
- youth/scout leaders

The following examples of helpful father-figures are largely self-explanatory.

Father-figures within the family

Grandparents

We believe it's important to step in and help with the grandchildren and spend time with them whilst our son is getting himself set up. In any case if I get an invitation to go out I think to myself, "Well, my 4 year old granddaughter is wiser and prettier than those people so I think I would prefer to spend my evening with her".

Sir Michael Parkinson – multi award-winning British talk show host and author, Bray

Uncles

> My mother's brother, my uncle Grant, was very important in my life. He was wonderful to me. He was warm and funny as well as being supporting and loving.
>
> I always knew he was there for me.
>
> He was not like my dad at all.

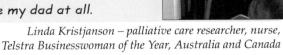

Linda Kristjanson – palliative care researcher, nurse, Telstra Businesswoman of the Year, Australia and Canada

Stepfathers

Whilst stepfathers are not as effective as natural dads at influencing adolescent girls,[8] a nurturing, non-conflictual stepfather can clearly improve adolescent well-being.[9,10]

A low point was when my 16 year old stepdaughter ran away from home. It's been a difficult life for her with her father having basically abandoned her.

I've never been able to fill the gap. In fact I know I can't fill that hole because she needs me, but not as a dad - she needs her natural dad. What she needs from me is to be a friend and I have tried to do that although, to be honest, she was the oldest and copped the most of my mistakes early on.

Peter de Blanc – soldier, biker, IT consultant, Wembley

As a stepfather I made it clear to the girls the following: I am not your father. You have a father. I am not trying to replace your father, but I love your mum and I will be staying here with her and with you. I just hope, at the end of the day, that I will be considered one of your friends.

Tim Willoughby – Olympian, America's Cup yachtsman, stockbroker, Perth

Community father-figures

One of the simplest yet most effective ways for you as a dad to become a helpful father-figure is to change the way you relate to your children's friends and to your nieces. You are a father-figure to them and you could think about following most of the suggestions in this book with those children.

> We talk about the double-duty dad. Fathers who are already doing a good job with their own kids should think about other kids. They can either integrate other kids into their current lives or, when the kids are grown up and leave they can invest back with other kids.

Roland Warren – President, US National Fatherhood Initiative, Washington DC

> Not only did I work hard with my own kids but I used to like to talk to other kids who would come down the street and talk to us, particularly kids from split families.

Brian Edwards – physiotherapist, pilot, vigneron, author, Margaret River

> I had four male mentors when I was a teenager, particularly Stan Nichols who ran one of Frank Sedgman's gyms and treated me like one of his own children. All of these mentors believed in me much more than I did in myself. In the end they showed enough confidence in me that, despite my lack of confidence in myself, I believed them.

Margaret Court – tennis champion, 62 Grand Slam titles, pastor, Perth

Parents of a friend

I had a friend when I was 16, named Jane. I loved going to her house because she lived in the country and had horses and her family were so friendly. In fact they easily accepted me and I came to really love them (I still do!).

What I remember about her dad Peter was that he used to give me great big bear hugs when I arrived.

Because I didn't have a dad he was the only man to do this (my grandpa only gave me a kiss on the cheek).

It used to unnerve me. It made me feel a little embarrassed but I believe it was crucial to my development at that time. As a teenage girl I needed the physical touch and affirmation given safely by a father-figure and I was lucky to have it.

Sarah Mumford – social worker, London

Schoolteachers

Male teachers are in a powerful position to act as father-figures for children.

Without too much effort they could have a big impact on these children, especially those without fathers, and especially if they can create one-on-one times with the kids, even during class time.

But for the same reason they can also be a powerful negative force too.

Jim Watterston – Director, Department of Education and Early Childhood Development, Melbourne

Pastors and priests

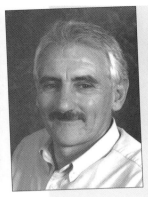

My local parish priest, Father Cunningham, remains one of the most significant 'influencers' in my life.

His unconditional love; his gentle strength; his willingness to roll up his sleeves and work in the community; and, his authentic love and respect for all kids was 'safe' for me as a kid and inspirational as an adult.

As a kid I longed for love from my Dad, but he was unable to express or give that; Father Cunningham did.

Father Cunningham often made me feel like the most important and special kid in the world.

Peter Prout – farmer, soldier, lecturer in Education, teacher, pastor, Subiaco

Dad's friends

My Uncle Harry was a lovely man. He wasn't really my uncle, he was a man that my father had met just after the war.

Like my own father he carried his own baggage and was battling his own demons from that.

But he has always been a special person to me.

Susan Timmis – art teacher, London

I need to re-emphasise that anyone who is a father-figure in a girl's life can, when they read the word 'father' in this book, think about themselves as 'father-figures' – virtually everything said in this book applies to father-figures as much as to dads.

I wish I had the space to tell all the stories of women I spoke to whose lives were changed because they had a wonderful father-figure.

Summary
What father-figures can do

- intentionally make all your contacts with nieces & your children's friends encouraging
- take other kids along with yours to the football, camping, dinner or movies
- be interested - tell them how special they are
- seek out other father-figures for your own kids
- encourage sole-parent mothers to consider appropriate father-figures for their children

CLINICAL TESTING HAD CONFIRMED THAT THE iDAD™ DELIVERED UP TO 240% BETTER FATHERING THAN THE AVERAGE MALE. TONY FELT THIS WAS THE BEST FATHERING DECISION HE HAD EVER MADE. IT WAS A REAL INVESTMENT IN HIS DAUGHTER AND HE COULD NOW GET ON WITH MORE IMPORTANT THINGS.

Fathers should tell their daughters that they are beautiful. If a father says it, a daughter believes it.

My father never said it, so when others said it to me throughout my life I thought they were just being kind.

It is only the last couple of years, and I'm now in my fifties, that I have started to believe it.

If your father doesn't tell you that you are beautiful, it takes a long time before you believe it.

Linda Carlson – actor, New York and Hollywood

Chapter 3

Helping a girl feel beautiful

"A daughter first looks to her father for the message that she is beautiful"

CHAPTER TOPICS

- Why it is important to help a girl feel beautiful
- Affirming outer beauty and inner beauty
- Relationship between sexuality and beauty
- The power of media messages
- Affirming her attractiveness in teenage years

Why it is important to help a girl feel beautiful

The signals that girls get concerning their beauty when they are young can have a life-long influence on whether they can ever see themselves as being beautiful.[1]

Fathers have a major influence on whether daughters feel attractive and beautiful or not.[2,3] When she gets to the age when she says 'Mirror, mirror on the wall, am I beautiful at all?', dads are that first mirror.

The media has a profound effect on a girl's sense of what beauty is, and in the process can make girls feel unattractive.[4,5] Fathers have been shown to be a powerful force to counteract that influence and help a girl feel beautiful.[2,3] Father-figures such as grandfathers have also been shown to be effective in this regard.[6]

Our daughters can't all look like movie stars. In fact very few women do. But they are looking for feedback from their dads on the issue of beauty.

> When a girl gets to the age when she says 'Mirror, mirror on the wall, am I beautiful at all?', dads are that first mirror

And our daughters don't have the bodies of models either. When I look at the mannequins in shop windows I see shapes that I don't see in the street. Women in the real world just don't look like the women in shop windows, on TV or in magazines. The advertising industry spends over $5 billion per year using such images to tell women that they are not attractive enough so it is no wonder our daughters struggle to feel attractive.[7]

It can start with Barbie Dolls, then TV advertising pushes a specific notion of beauty. Then girls get exposed to magazines which maintain that notion. As the Barbies, TV and magazines have their effects, peer pressure reinforces that message on a daily basis.

Our girls are being influenced by forces outside our control to make them think they are not attractive.

Do you want TV advertisers to determine what your own daughter thinks of herself or do you want to have a say in that?

This is an enormous pressure on girls, fitting a particular image of 'prettiness'.[8] Fathers are well placed to counter that pressure by communicating to their daughters a sense of their attractiveness. That can profoundly change how they feel about themselves and whether or not they need to go looking elsewhere to get those messages of attractiveness. It is equally important that fathers do not add to that pressure by making negative comments about their looks or by directly putting them down.

If you succeed in communicating this then your daughter will grow up to feel beautiful and will talk to the mirror on the wall rather than just listening to it.

I would like to emphasise that by attractiveness and beauty I do not mean 'being pretty'. Attractiveness does mean something physical but it is equally about their personality, their being. That means that they will remain attractive even if they lose their looks.

I read a Spike Milligan poem years ago when I was a backpacker which captures what I am getting at. The poem is called 'Mirror, Mirror'.

> A young Spring tender girl combed her joyous hair.
> 'You are very ugly,' said the mirror.
> But on her young lips hung a smile of dove-secret loveliness. For only that morning, had not the blind boy said 'You are beautiful'?

Spike Milligan – comedian[9]

The reason why dads are so well placed to make a girl feel beautiful is that he is the first man in her life, the first significant non-female that she encounters.

There is no doubt, dads, that what we say about her beauty will have a profound effect on our daughters. Mums are important in this regard, but dads are very powerful in giving messages of attractiveness. This is well described in the published literature[2,3,10-13] and by all of the women I interviewed. Dads are the first and most important source of information that daughters refer to in order to find out if they are attractive. Girls 'have their radar out' for this validation.

> When a dad tells a little girl she is wonderful it means a lot more than when a mum does it because when mums do it it's just expected.

Peta Fong – hairdresser, City Beach

Because of this sensitivity to external validation outside the female gender, fathers are in the front line for giving male feedback. It is not something we dads can avoid. She is looking for those signals from us and if we don't give any feedback we leave a void. That means we can't opt out with an excuse like 'I am just not a very affirming person'.

> Young girls are very attentive to all the signals a father gives them. They are looking for this from their father.
>
> Men should not take this lightly.
>
> It is not just the verbal but the non verbal that is being read by young women.
>
> It is true that fathers and father-figures can have a powerful role in the way a woman lives, in both positive and negative ways. It's a young woman's first exposure to what a good man can be.

Linda Kristjanson – palliative care researcher, nurse, Telstra Businesswoman of the Year, Australia and Canada

If you don't do these things, at a minimum your daughter may grow up being uncertain of her attractiveness.[14] So many beautiful women feel unattractive throughout their lives because their fathers did not affirm their beauty. I have met many women whose fathers made them feel so beautiful and special that they grew up with a confidence and personal radiance that made people love to be with them.

> **Many beautiful women always feel unattractive because their fathers did not affirm their beauty**

Failure to affirm our daughters can also cause them to search for affirmation from other men which can lead to multiple unfulfilling and/or risky sexual encounters. This process is well described in the literature and discussed later - girls search for affirmation from boys because they did not get it from their dads.[15-20]

Affirm her outer beauty

Beauty can be outer and inner. If you get used to thinking like that you will recognise beauty where you never saw it before. Then you might also realise that there is no real ugliness, just different types of beauty.

Let's talk about a daughter's outer appearance, as distinct from her inner beauty. She does want to know that she is externally beautiful.

The word beautiful is better than the word pretty. She might be pretty, but I don't think we should overemphasise that. If she grows up 'trading on her looks', she is already disadvantaged. Those looks will disappear and, in any case, she needs to know, within herself, that her beauty is more than that. But we do need to give our daughters feedback on their outer beauty.

> *Fathers need to not be scared about giving their daughters comments about their physical appearance.*
>
> *I want my daughter Gemma's worth to be in who she is, not what she looks like, that is true and clear.*
>
> *But women want to know they look nice.*
>
> *That need can't be ignored. It's important.*

Rosemary Kendell – occupational therapist, Floreat

There will be other ways in which her appearance is beautiful, whether she is pretty or not in the traditional social sense. There will be things about her looks that you can reinforce, such as:

There is no real ugliness, just different types of beauty

 a smile that warms your heart and lights up the room

 eyes that are inquisitive, insightful, beautiful, compassionate and sparkle

 laughter that brightens up the world

There are many other things too, I am sure, that you could find to comment on if you put your mind and eyes to the job.

All daughters need their outer beauty affirmed. If you have two daughters and one is prettier, in the traditional sense, and gets lots of positive feedback, the other one will watch carefully for how people react to her, especially how men react and especially how her father reacts. That is why it is important to make all daughters feel equally attractive.

It is not appropriate to try to get out of that situation by saying one daughter has the looks and the other has the brains. That pigeon-holes them – the bright one might feel ugly and the pretty one may give up learning things because she thinks she is stupid. They both need their beauty and capacity for learning to be equally encouraged.

It is important to make all daughters feel equally attractive.

Remind them that they are special in their appearance, that there are uniquely attractive things about their looks. Think of the Mona Lisa – the woman in the painting is not a stunningly attractive woman but that painting is certainly special.

Compliment her on how she is dressed

Girls adorn themselves in various ways, with clothes, shoes, jewellery, hair etc. This is not a trivial exercise for them. They want feedback on how it makes them look. It is important that dads are involved in that and that we are sensitive about what we say.

When she dresses up, comment on how beautiful she looks. That is part of the feeling of outer beauty a woman can experience.

For daughters, it is really important that fathers compliment them on their appearance and presentation.

Geraldine Doogue – *TV presenter, journalist, author, Sydney*

Use compliments that are positive but believable

When it comes to commenting on beauty, exaggerating has its problems. Kids can smell a rat. It is more believable if you are more specific. Truly look at them and don't be glib.

Daughters need to know they can't be the prettiest but they all want to look nice.

Compliments from Dad about hair, clothes, etc carry an enormous weight.

Rosemary Kendell – *occupational therapist, Floreat*

Affirm her inner beauty

Her inner beauty is also important to reinforce, because it makes her sense of worth and attractiveness increase. It will be about her and also about what she does. In some ways this is richer.

One of the most wonderful things a father can give a daughter is affirmation.

He can do that by consistently speaking encouraging, affirming, appreciative words to her, commenting not only on the way she looks but more importantly on who she is and what she does

*Sila Lee – author and co-founder of
The Marriage Course, London*

There is a wonderful scene in the movie "Little Miss Sunshine" where a young girl's grandfather reassures her she is beautiful inside and out.[21]

Olive: *Grandpa, am I pretty?*

Grandpa: *Olive, you are the most beautiful girl in the whole world.*

Olive: *Nah, you're just saying that.*

Grandpa: *No! I'm madly in love with you and it's not because of your brains or your personality. You're beautiful inside and out.*

Some words to use that might affirm her inner beauty include:

- 'I love the way you are such a kind friend to others, always there to help'
- 'I love the way you make friends with unpopular kids and new kids at your school'
- 'those birthday cards you make for people really give them a lift'
- 'I admire your curiosity, compassion and honesty'

Dads and father-figures, I encourage you to look for things other than her appearance to compliment.

> How a father acts towards his daughter determines to a large extent how she develops. Fathers need to not just focus on how she looks, but other things that she does well, for example athletics, school work or any of her interests really.
>
> If he focuses only on her being pretty that may be what she accepts as her place in life and she may not strive for more than that.

Sharon Greenberg – occupational therapist, Seattle

Summary
Affirming beauty

- reinforce things that don't involve 'prettiness', such as her smile, her eyes and her laugh

- even if she is pretty, don't overemphasise it

- make your compliments believable

- acknowledge her inner beauty (her heart, mind, kindness, creativity etc)

Beauty when teenage hormones are raging

This feedback about beauty from fathers is especially important when your daughter enters teenage years. This is because it is at that time that she is most sensitive to external signals of acceptance and attractiveness. It seems like a cruel irony that just when she is most worried about friends, acceptance and appearance she is emotionally more labile, breaks out in zits, requires braces on her teeth, her breasts start bulging and she starts the sometimes embarrassing process of menstruation.

My wife Jacqui told me early on in our marriage that she felt that her dad had unintentionally but noticeably withdrawn his love and affirmation from her when she became a teenager and she felt it badly. A number of other women have told me similar stories. I was therefore on the lookout myself not to do the same thing when Amy entered adolescence. I am trying to get this right, although it is hard to be sure.

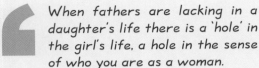

Dads, don't stop affirming and hugging your daughter during adolescence

So dads, don't stop affirming her beauty when she is a teenager. Don't abandon her at this time. Go out of your way to tell her how beautiful she is during this period.

When fathers are lacking in a daughter's life there is a 'hole' in the girl's life, a hole in the sense of who you are as a woman.

This is especially the case for adolescents because so much of adolescence is about who you are as a woman and a father can be very important in defining that.

Yvonne de Blanc – social worker, Wembley

Women who are made to feel genuinely affirmed as beautiful are often relaxed socially whereas those who are pretty but who feel insecure can spend a lot of the time worrying about what others think of them. Sometimes people who feel attractive in themselves are more likely to reach out to others whereas people with a low view of themselves can tend to see the world in relation to their self-esteem – they put others down to reduce the perceived gap or they react with envy when others receive praise.

> If you can engender a feeling of true beauty in your daughter you will be giving her a strong foundation in life

So dads, if you can engender a feeling of true beauty in your daughter you will be giving her a strong foundation in life.

To be liked because of inner beauty and genuineness is a real gift.

And it is helpful to make clear to a daughter that any man who doesn't appreciate those aspects of her looks and character does not deserve her.

What if your daughter has a physical impairment that affects her attractiveness?

All parents have to deal with temporary perceptions of unattractiveness sometimes, e.g. when acne and braces are an issue.[22] The challenge to convince a daughter that she is beautiful if she has some sort of physical impairment is harder and lies squarely at the feet of her family. Dads, we have a major role in this. As is the case for many of these sorts of issues, we do not have the only role but we do have a major role.

The whole of society is geared towards seeing beauty as something positive and ugliness as something negative or even evil and there is some evidence to support the idea that fathers and others behave differently towards kids who are not as attractive as others.[23]

The programming begins early in life when children are exposed to seemingly innocuous stories such as The Ugly Duckling and Rudolph the Red Nosed Reindeer. Snow White's wall mirror had to tell who was the prettiest person and the evil person in that story was the ugly one. In Cinderella, the ugly sisters were the evil ones. Often in television shows and movies, the good guys are handsome and the bad guys are ugly. This is common. It is not surprising therefore that children who have some kind of defect are easily rejected.

The comedian Wendy Harmer describes how, when she was growing up with a bilateral cleft palate, her father never shied away from that fact but tried to help her overcome her fears. I was quite moved by her description of how he tried to help her.

> Even though I had a bilateral cleft palate my father would make me stand up and read in front of people.
>
> When I talked to him about it later he explained how he had to make me strong.
>
> He said to me, "Don't you think it hurt me? It broke my heart to have to get you to do that."
>
> Then we both cried about it together.
>
> He is incredibly proud of me and I love him very much.

Wendy Harmer – comedian, Melbourne[24]

Some problems are not small. If your child has a significant physical problem then you have a job to do. Although the ugly duckling had to change to get acceptance, your daughter does not. She is already beautiful. She will need to learn to see herself as beautiful in other ways and to love that ugly duckling.

The way to do that is described above. Find things about her external beauty that you genuinely think are praiseworthy, her eyes, her smile, her laughter, her facial structure, her hair, her clothing or her jewellery. Then focus on her inner beauty and find all the things that make her beautiful inside, and keep telling her, especially when she falters in her belief in them (e.g. after a bad day in the school playground).

Part of this process is to respond to her equally compared to the other kids in your family.

Other ideas that have worked include offering solutions (e.g. to see a dermatologist about acne) to be careful at sensitive times not to criticise minor things that seem innocuous, to give occasional pick-me-ups (e.g. shows, events, clothes) and to be willing to get professional help.[25]

Establish a 'no put down' rule about appearance

If your daughter has a problem with weight, height or any other physical issue, make sure your family have a strict 'no put down' rule. Make your home a place where your daughter can know she is safe from the verbal barbs of the schoolyard.

> **Make sure that you and the rest of your family have a strict 'no put down' rule**

Also, teach her things to say at school to anyone who teases her – a kind but affirming reply at school, especially a humorous one, is better than an aggressive response, running away or giving up.

If this is done well she will not only get through this OK but her problem might even become a strength for her, something she learns to laugh at and which generates respectful humour in others as she refuses to shy away from it. I have met people who are like that and I really admire them.

Sexuality as part of her beauty

It might be a surprise to some dads to realise that we should not avoid appropriately acknowledging positive sexuality in our daughter's attractiveness. Appropriate and safe acknowledgement of sexuality is helpful to daughters.[26] Don't let the fact that you are from the opposite gender stop you mentioning sexuality in a positive way.

Although it may be difficult, fathers also need to acknowledge a girl's sexuality.

Carol Gisselquist – Higher Education Associate,
Pennsylvania Department of Education

The father-daughter relationship is critical.

But it is not related so much to modelling, as it is with the son, but to positive affirmation regarding the femininity of the daughter that the father provides.

This is one of the critical roles that fathers have with daughters.

James Dobson – psychologist, author, founder of
Focus on the Family, Colorado Springs

Teaching her about physical beauty and sexuality

As you remind her that she is attractive, and compliment her clothes and hair, you could consider talking with her about the social impact of her physical beauty. For example you could remind her that how she dresses partly determines how boys will look her. If she dresses in an alluring way in order to get the attention of boys she will get boys responding that way. That's because she has invited them to. She should be proud of her body and of her sexuality, but if boys respond to her as an object rather than as a person then they are the not respecting her. She does have some control over whether males look at her with respect or not. What does she really want?

> *Fathers have a role in teaching their daughters that they should not be treated as an object ie. not objectified.*
>
> *For example what a daughter wears can cause a man to look at her as an object.*
>
> *Girls need to understand that.*

Sam Brownback – US Senator, Presidential candidate, Kansas

It helps if she is not naive about the reactions she invites. I need to emphasize here that the way a woman dresses in no way diminishes a male's responsibility to act respectfully to that woman, regardless of how she looks.

Dads have an important role in helping a daughter form a healthy view of her own body image

A girl's sense of body beauty, and the effect of the media on that sense, start early for girls, e.g. before age 11.[27] By middle school, 40% of girls say they are too fat and 30% are dieting and by high school, 50% of girls try to lose weight.[28] Also young girls say that they are more afraid of becoming fat than they are of cancer, nuclear war, or losing their parents.[28] Whilst the obesity epidemic means that some of this is appropriate,[28] it can also lead to a distorted concept of body shape that contributes to eating disorders.

The affirmation and acceptance of the girl's physical beauty by a father profoundly affects whether his daughter feels beautiful or awkward. This includes her sense of her body. She is looking to dad to get a signal about how her body looks.

Because her peers and the TV are shouting out messages to her, dads need to be aware of affirming their daughter's body beauty. Failure to do this puts her at greater risk of having an eating disorder.[29,30]

There is a clear association between a father's attitude to his daughter's physical attractiveness and her perceptions of the need to be slimmer, and thus her dieting behaviour.[29]

The role of the father in the cause and management of eating disorders in girls is important but has largely been ignored until recently. Fathers who are less controlling and who build confidence are most effective at helping a girl love her body, reducing her risk of eating disorders.[22, 31-36]

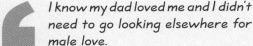

The role of the father in the cause and management of eating disorders in girls is important

Whilst mothers will often do whatever they can to help their daughter feel good about her body, daughters also need those signals from their dads. This helps her feel physically attractive and worthwhile and less worried about rejection by her peers.[37]

Feeling beautiful and relating to men as friends

I know my dad loved me and I didn't need to go looking elsewhere for male love.

I have noticed that women who grow up without good close relationships with their fathers are a bit insecure.

They end up talking about how they look and how they feel about themselves and they talk about boys all the time.

Catharine Ryun – White House staffer, daughter of Congressman Ryun, Washington DC

If you succeed in making your daughter aware of how beautiful she is she has a greater chance of becoming confident with men as friends, independent of any romantic link. This is partly because she will not always need to have her 'man radar' out trying to get signals that she is attractive. She will be more likely to feel comfortable with her body and her sexuality without having to have that continually reinforced by males.

I look at my own daughter and I see that she has emerged an extremely confident young woman. Confident in herself as an attractive, sexual being who is comfortable with men as well as women.

She has been heavily helped by the two most important men in her life, her father and her stepfather.

That does leave me with a bit of a sense of regret in terms of what my own father could have given me.

Geraldine Doogue – TV presenter, journalist, author, Sydney

Keep affirming her and she won't need a 'man radar' to get signals of her worth

And this will mean that she, unlike so many young women, will not seek to get her identity from males. This is very important. You must have met women who seem to have no identity when they are by themselves, but only feel significant when they are with males. They are often asking those males the question, without using words, that they asked of their dads, 'mirror mirror on the wall, am I attractive at all?' To fail to deliver that answer to girls is to risk them having unmet needs in their relationships with males.

My father gave me confidence in myself as a woman and made it very clear that I should not get my identity from boys. "You just can't get your own identity that way," he said.

Bryn Freedman – author, managing news editor, Los Angeles

When girls spend time with a father who tries to understand them and who values them, they feel secure in themselves and a bond is created which means she doesn't have to look for frivolous relationships to fill in the void left by a father who doesn't do these things.

Danae Dobson – author, daughter of James Dobson, Pasadena

Help her think through manipulative advertising because magazine and TV ads often create the illusion that women are only sexual objects, not people.[38-43] So teach your daughter to recognise that. Help her to understand how TV advertisements are pitched to sell things. It would be very troubling for advertisers if the entire female viewing audience thought for themselves and critiqued all advertisements.

One good way to do this is to turn the sound off and try to guess who they are aiming the advertisements at – it is strangely very simple when the sounds are turned down to do that. A good strategy is to get them to laugh at these techniques rather than developing an anti-advertiser vendetta.

Quiz Question

Who said: "Beauty is how you feel inside, and it reflects in your eyes. It is not something physical."?

Answer: Sophia Loren – Italian film actress, b.1934

Summary
Some reasons why a girl might feel unattractive

- TV and magazine advertising made her feel that she is unattractive unless she buys a particular product, yet that product doesn't change things for her
- This message has reinforced by Barbie Dolls then peer pressure
- her father added to that pressure with negative rather than positive comments
- she has confused attractiveness and beauty with 'being pretty'
- more compliments were given to her prettier sister
- she, and her father, have never appreciated 'inner beauty'
- she has been made to feel that her sexual beauty is bad
- she has been made to hate her body shape by 'put downs'
- other males in her life have never thought to affirm her beauty

A girl and her beauty
– some extra things to think about

Dads

- tell your daughter repeatedly how beautiful she is
- affirm her outer and inner beauty
- make special efforts when she is a teenager
- teach her about physical beauty in the context of sexuality and its social effects
- help her to think through manipulative advertising

Adult daughters

- ask yourself if you often feel unattractive
- think about how much of that feeling comes from the signals you did or didn't receive from your father
- discuss with your husband if that feeling impacts on your relationship, e.g. your receptivity to affirmation

Husbands

- be willing to listen if your partner's sense of attractiveness doesn't relate to what you say but how she has been programmed to think of herself
- think about ways in which you can affirm her beauty, inside and out

Father-figures

- continually remind a girl of how beautiful she is, inside and out

- only do so in appropriate ways and situations

- especially do that if she has no dad around or if her biological dad isn't doing this

Is lack of confidence a girl thing? I am not sure. I can say to my daughters "you're great", but that is not enough. If Tony says it, it seems to have a greater effect.

I don't know whether that is because it is a girl thing, i.e. the need for validation from a male, or simply because he doesn't say it as often so it has more impact.

Fiona Wood – plastic surgeon, Australian of the Year, Perth

Chapter 4

Building up a daughter's confidence

"Fathers can help make, or break, a girl's confidence in herself"

CHAPTER TOPICS

- Why it is important for fathers and father-figures to build, not destroy, a girl's confidence
- Independence versus helplessness
- Handling mistakes, failures and risks
- How to discipline without destroying confidence
- Confidence and service

Why it is important for fathers and father-figures to build, not destroy, a girl's confidence

It was my father who gave me confidence when I was a child.

He never put me under pressure to perform and encouraged me in all the things I did, particularly the things that I enjoyed.

Alison Pocock – magistrate, Milton Keynes

Whilst both parents are important in the generation of confidence in daughters,[1] fathers seem to have a particularly strong effect, starting at a young age.[2-12] Father-figures can also be powerful in developing confidence and self-efficacy in women.[5]

Early on this confidence has a measurable effect on her school performance,[6] then later, on her life choices. She feels more able to make career decisions based on independence and self-reliance, she is free to choose what she wants to do free of pressure from peers and she is less constrained by gender stereotyping, including being a homemaker by choice.[7,8]

> Confidence means feeling capable, but not self-important

Confidence is the belief that she can do things and that the things that she does will actually have an effect in the world. It means that she has belief in her abilities, has some control over her life and can shape her future.[9]

Confidence is not an inflated sense of self-importance or the idea that the world owes her something, or that she is entitled to anything she wants. But confidence means that she can make choices and that those choices will mean something.

In my interviews I found many adult daughters who described how the confidence that they had in their lives stemmed from their relationship with their father.

I have also met many women who said that no matter how well they did in their careers, their father never seemed to believe in them or have any confidence in them.

If I volunteered to clear the dishes and wipe the table after dinner, my father would not thank me for the effort or praise me for 'doing more.' Instead, he would more likely say: "You missed a spot."

I grew up feeling like I could not please him.

I still feel like I am bound to disappoint anyone with expectations of me, because I never felt that I could please my father.

Carol Gisselquist – Higher Education Associate, Pennsylvania Department of Education

I have met many women whose fathers have been absent or critical and these women live lives of uncertainty.

Gay Crooks – paediatric cancer specialist & scientist, Los Angeles

My wife also noticed something intriguingly similar some years ago and pointed it out to me. She had just heard a number of prominent, successful women interviewed on a morning talkback show and she noticed that all of them had identified a close, confidence-building relationship with their father was the main thing that gave them the confidence to go on and succeed in life.

It is important to think about these things because some dads are still stuck with a 'heroic knight' notion, whereby they want to express their love for their daughter by protecting her all the time. Whilst this might be true when she is young, gradually she will need dad to help her become independent, to give her the confidence to look after herself.[10,11]

I think women often need more encouragement than men, who often seem to have a natural self-confidence.

Theresa May – *Chairman of the Conservative Party of Great Britain, London*

Giving a daughter confidence without making her self-centred

Some fathers and mothers worry that giving a daughter confidence may make her feel self-important, that she is more important than everyone else around her. But an appearance of confidence often comes from a deep lack of it, a kind of social 'bluff'. Nevertheless it is vital to mention here that the process of making a child feel confident and intrinsically important requires us to help her value others also.

Confidence is a tricky thing. It is important to give children a sense of confidence in their ability to have a go at things.
There's a difference between making a girl feel valued and feeling self important.
I'm talking about making girls feeling valued as a person, not more important than anyone else.
Of course that needs to come from the mother as well.

Carmen Lawrence – *President of the Australian Labor Party, Federal Member for Fremantle*

What if dads fail to give their daughters confidence?

> *Am I confident?*
>
> *To some extent. I had to learn it.*
>
> *I think if you grow up unconfident but then get married, have children and some success you can shed a lot of those insecurities.*
>
> *I know that I would have been different if my father had given me that confidence.*

Geraldine Doogue – TV presenter, journalist, author, Sydney

I don't want any dads who are reading this to imagine that it is optional. Girls really do get a strong sense of confidence from their fathers so what worries me is that if I fail as a dad to do this I can profoundly influence my daughter's future life. She may still be successful outwardly, but never feel like she is genuinely successful. I have seen that many times in my own profession – successful women lacking confidence because of how they were treated, usually by their fathers, when they were young. Here is one example that a medical colleague of mine told me which illustrates this:

> *A brilliant friend of mine died recently of breast cancer. Despite all the international success that she experienced, she never really felt confident in herself.*
>
> *I learnt that her lack of confidence in life probably stemmed from her relationship with her father - he never gave her the message that she was worthwhile. That was the message that she really wanted to hear from him.*

Charis Jennings – physician, London

Belief in a daughter's ability can cause her to strive for what she is good at rather than spend years without that confidence.[12] If her father has denied her that encouragement it can take a long time for a daughter to become confident or at least to find her place in life.

> My dad's lack of praise and encouragement affected me for a while but I eventually found what I really enjoy doing.
>
> I spent 10 years teaching and really it just took me that long to find out what I really wanted to do. Then I became a TV producer and really found my niche.

Susie Annus – TV producer, Perth

So dads, given that it is important to impart confidence in girls, how can we do that? Here are some ideas.

Avoid letting her develop total dependence on males

Being confident as a woman means that she doesn't become dependent on males. Don't reinforce any notion that only a man will be able to rescue her – she can rescue herself. Have you noticed how in many of the classic fairytales it is the woman who is helpless? Sleeping Beauty needed a prince to wake her up – why didn't she just choose to wake herself up? Cinderella was rescued by Prince Charming, and on it goes.

In fact I have noticed the opposite in life – many men only really become awake and alive when they are in a close relationship with a woman, one who can draw them out, even rescue them. Some mums talk to their daughters about avoiding being a stereotypically 'helpless female' but dads should also talk about this with their daughters.

So dads, fix things together with her. If her bicycle tyre needs mending, teach her how to fix it rather than always fixing it yourself.

Fathers and father-figures, invite girls to help you to do things that you might otherwise consider reserved for boys such as fixing household items, mowing the lawn, giving an opinion about a sporting event or building a garden shed.

They may not choose to do these things, but give them the same options as you would give the boys.

> It is important that daughters are not stereotyped by their fathers. For example one man I met treated his daughter completely differently to his son - he talked to her in a baby voice and only did girly things with her.
>
> He overdid it, treating her as being delicate and giving her a signal that she was incapable of doing what her brother could do.

Shane Gould – triple Olympic swimming gold medallist and world record holder, Margaret River

One of the reasons to do this is to avoid automatic role delineation in marriage, e.g. mum does the cooking but dad fixes things. Of course where there is mutually agreed division of tasks in marriage it is, of course, right to share them, but on a skills basis rather than on a gender basis.[13]

Another important component of developing confidence in a daughter is to treat her mother as being a capable person. If wives are required to submit passively to a man, that role models the idea that women should defer to men and that women should not strive to reach their potential. But if you have

> **Engendering confidence in a daughter includes treating her mother as being a capable person**

role-modelled the idea that you believe that the women in your life have the potential to do almost anything, your daughter is more likely to believe it.

Reinforce a confidence that is independent of gender

Girls also need to be told to take what opportunities come their way and not let the fact that they are a girl hold them back.

Peta Fong – hairdresser, City Beach

Whilst there are clear general biological differences between males and females, these differences are not universal for every person of each gender[14-16] – there are plenty of women who can read maps and fix things better than their male partners. We ought not to make her feel less than a woman if she can read maps – she can be proud of it *and* be feminine.

Giving confidence to your daughters and encouraging them probably should not include phrases like 'do it despite being a woman' or 'do it to prove women can do it'.

They should strive to achieve things *regardless* of gender, simply because it is the thing they want to do. Where it especially matters is when your daughter decides that she won't try something 'because she is a girl'.

It's important a father doesn't favour boys over girls or vice versa, but rather sees each child's unique personality and gifts and affirms these.

Sila Lee – author and co-founder, The Marriage Course, London

A father or father-figure can help a woman realise that she does not need to be deferential, passive, compliant or placid, asking permission if she is right (e.g. adding "don't you think?" to sentences).[17]

That is important for fathers to articulate. She doesn't have to remain at home doing the cooking and looking after the kids. Our daughters can be encouraged to do what they want to do. And although there are some disciplines that women find hard to break into, in general any profession is open to them now. For example in 1900 in the USA there were only 200 women doctors but now females form at least half of most medical schools.[18] Indeed, in the last 50 years of the 20th century the percentage of women in medicine, law and engineering rose from 6%, 3% and 1% to 25%, 28% and 10% respectively.[19]

Dads and father-figures can help correct any distorted gender notions that their daughters might acquire in society.

As dads we could try to remember to use terms correctly, such as 'police officer' instead of 'policeman'.

But she should also feel free to stay at home if she so chooses, as a positive choice not as a default position. Because so many mothers are in paid employment now, it takes a lot of confidence and courage for them to turn their backs on a career to stay at home for some years or to work part-time. Nowadays that decision requires as much personal confidence as the decision to change careers or seek another job.

> Dads and father-figures can help correct any distorted gender notions that their daughters might acquire in society.

If you can help your daughter through these issues she can become more confident, not needing to live in combat with the world, men or otherwise, in order for her femaleness to be accepted. She will not need to be self-effacing, passive, submissive and compliant and she will think for herself. She will be able to be assertive without being aggressive. She will be free to see kindness as a strength, not a weakness.

It is frustrating when it is only women who fight for equality of gender language and opportunity. This is a role well suited for dads and father-figures also. Men could stand up and do this, especially if they have a daughter.

Encourage her sense of humour – this builds confidence and resilience

> Daughters need a sense of humour from their fathers, a sense of the ridiculous.
>
> Why do they need that from the father rather than the mother?
>
> It could be both, but my father was important in helping me see the humour in things.

Pauline Dixon – social worker, Shenton Park

Another useful strategy is to deliberately help our daughters develop humour as a confidence-building social skill. This gives them resilience and a way of handing difficult situations.

> When we talk to the kids we always try to give them the confidence to speak up. For example we give them confidence to develop their humour by encouraging them to try it out on us, even if it's not funny.

Dennis Cometti – sports commentator, author, Perth

Confidence means giving her more independence

Part of her confidence building will be to encourage her to gradually establish independence from you, as her parents. It means giving her more and more freedom and, at the same time, teaching her to minimise risks. A young woman is safer if her father or father-figure teaches her how to avoid situations where she might be at risk of mugging, sexual assault or date rape – this reduces her risk of date victimisation and harm.[20]

And freedom does not mean an absence of limits. Indeed lack of limits increases kids risks and anxiety.[21-23] Freedom and trust mean setting clear boundaries but allowing them freedom within those boundaries, not micromanaging all their decisions. This system of providing strict boundaries but freedom to live within those boundaries reduces their risks of suffering the consequences of careless freedom (e.g. substance abuse).[23]

So as dads and father-figures we need to remind girls about the dangers of being out late at night when men are intoxicated, about avoiding dangerous situations such being alone in dark places, walking home late at night and being alone with a selfish male who has been drinking a lot of alcohol.

> **Freedom and trust mean setting clear boundaries but allowing them freedom within those boundaries**

Remind them about drink spiking – also known as 'date rape drugging'- i.e. placing of barbiturates in a girl's drink then undertaking non-consensual sex at a time when they lack decision-making facilities.[24,25] For example, remind her not to leave an unfinished drink lying around when going to the toilet.

The same thing applies to checking on the arrangements that are in place for parties that our daughters are attending. Ask questions like 'where is it?', 'what adult supervision is there going to be?', 'will there be alcohol or drugs there?', 'what is their phone number so that I can talk to the parents?', 'what time will it be finished?' Our kids used to tell us that none of the other kids parents were asking those questions, but we found that plenty of the other parents had indeed asked their kids the exact same questions. I guess we said that to our parents too. It ultimately makes children feel more secure and more confident, not less, to know you are concerned and that you have prepared them to think about these situations, even though they might find those questions annoying.

I think talking about these things in a rational way should make your daughter confident and wise without making her over-anxious.

Discover and encourage her particular skills

Don't push your daughters in one area alone that *you* think is their skill, but let them try a range of things and persist long enough for them to find out what their special skills really are. That will also help them to accept the things they are not good at.

> *My advice to young dads would be to not get frustrated if your children don't share your ideals and enthusiasm, the areas that you want them to excel at. They may well excel at something else. Pushing them is an error.*

> *Craig Serjeant – Australian Test cricket vice-captain, investment-advisor, pharmacist, City Beach*

> *He's a sportsman, but my dad was at every drama performance I ever did, every music performance I ever did. Even though, I guess he probably didn't enjoy some of them he was always there supporting me at those things, things that he possibly couldn't identify with.*

> *Shari Serjeant – student, daughter of Craig*

This issue becomes even more important if there is a major differential between children in their abilities. But it has been shown that dads are really important in generating positive outcomes for kids with problems such as physical disabilities[26] or attention deficit disorder.[27]

Show her that you believe in her ability to make her own career choices

My father was a Professor of Microbiology - he was a virologist. He and I were very close and we got closer as we got older.
He believed in me and he always encouraged me to do what I really wanted to do myself.

Fiona Stanley – scientist, Director of the Telethon Institute for
Child Health Research, Australian of the Year, Nedlands

One clear way that dads and father-figures can give girls confidence and show belief in them is how they handle the process of making career choices.

My father gave me the message that he was confident of my future.
When I was studying a PhD in Psychology I decided to leave and take a job as a journalist in radio and television.
I was concerned that he would be disappointed but he said, "No. Go for it. Follow your passions and take risks. Don't worry. just go ahead and jump."

Bryn Freedman – author, managing news editor, Los Angeles

The phrase 'your wound is your gift' can be true. When I realised I was different from what my father expected of me I realised I would have to make it on my own. So I left home when I was young and went to acting school in New York City. He didn't really understand and I think would rather that I had settled down in the suburbs.
But I had to make that decision.
It would have been nice if he had said to me 'go for it. you can do it'.

Linda Carlson – actor, New York and Hollywood

Encourage a healthy view of competition

Confidence also involves competing. But there is a difference between competence (i.e. being able to do something well), competitiveness (i.e. doing something better than someone else) and confidence (i.e. being willing to have a go at things and to expect that your efforts will produce fruit).

Being too competitive makes girls feel unsuccessful unless they are winning, i.e. they require something external, a victory, to validate their worth.

Confidence and competence are independent of winning – girls should learn that they don't need someone else, or a scoreboard, to tell them that they are a capable person.

One study showed that fathers are important in developing healthy competition and reasonable risk-taking in girls, whereas mothers are important in developing nurturing, comforting skills.[28]

Modern society is highly competitive and Hollywood is just the same.

That means that time with kids competes with time at work.

It also has another negative side effect - kids become part of that competition. When that happens they become part of the parents' competitiveness, helping to fulfil their parents ideals.

I have always encouraged my kids to be themselves, not reflections of myself. As part of that I encourage them not to enter the world of show business.

Frank Pierson – Oscar winning screenwriter-director, Los Angeles

Encourage realistic goal-setting

Dads can have a role in helping daughters set goals for themselves, but goals which reflect their ability. These goals need to be achievable or else they will destroy their confidence.

> *Dad encouraged me to do things that I wouldn't otherwise do and this helped to make me feel competent. He would set challenges but help me to achieve them.*
>
> *Once we were at a creek which flowed into the ocean and dad challenged us to swim out to a tree branch that was in the middle of the creek. There was a strong current and I started to swim across, but I didn't think I could do it so I gave up and turned back. But he encouraged me and told me I could do it.*
>
> *I was terrified, but when he assured me that I could do it I received confidence from him and I did it.*
>
> *Then when I was around 14-15 years old I had one world swimming record to go that I hadn't broken - Dawn Fraser's 100m world record.*
>
> *He believed I could do it and that helped me believe I could do it. And I did it.*
>
> *He always set a challenge that was achievable and he always made me believe I could do it.*
>
> Shane Gould – triple Olympic swimming gold medallist
> and world record holder, Margaret River

Don't try to get success by always indicating you aren't satisfied

Some dads, like football coaches, try to get their children to continually strive to attain higher goals by indicating that they are never satisfied with them. But this has more chance of destroying confidence than building it up.

I often felt that my father was never satisfied with me. I think it was really that he didn't know how to praise me for the things I did.
He was always pushing me onto the next thing.

Lynda Green – teacher, Brighton

Avoid the use of sarcasm to get results

I am surprised at how often I hear fathers use goading or sarcasm when they talk with their daughters. Sometimes that is a selfish expression of the father's own emotions but often it comes from a desire to prompt the daughter into action.

> It can take a long time for a daughter to overcome lack of confidence caused by her father

The reason this approach is risky is that you can make things worse. If she has a tendency to low self esteem she will think that your sarcasm is true and that she has failed, supporting the notion that she is indeed a failure as a person. So you achieve the opposite result. Give confidence by encouragement, not by sarcasm and humiliation. Some girls are particularly sensitive to criticism from dad, even by nuance.

My dad was the only male in the house and he didn't know how to relate to females. My husband commented on the femininity of our house the first time he encountered it.
For example, our 'female radars' were finely tuned to nuances of feeling - our radars were out for any criticism, any hurting, any incident where we were being made fun of.

Brenda Hodges – teacher, Sydney

Teach her that confidence is an attitude

One of the things I learnt from a sports psychologist when I was a varsity football coach was the phrase 'whether you think you can, or whether you think you can't, you're right'. I have noticed that to be the case in many areas of life. Why not try that approach with your daughters.

Give her confidence that success is not out of her reach. The key to giving a daughter confidence is to always make it clear that you believe in her.

> *Girls also need for their fathers to believe in them. Pete has always shown great belief in the girls. That means they are really confident now.*

Sue LeSouef – nurse and lawyer, Nedlands

Confidence to lead

There are many situations in which women struggle to get leadership positions, though fortunately many fewer now than 30 years ago. When asking why there are so few eminent women, Silverman discovered that girls were just missing encouragement and guidance from fathers.[29,30] Indeed the father-daughter relationship has been shown in other studies to be an important factor in helping girls reach their full potential and develop leadership skills.[31]

If we keep telling our daughters that we believe in them they are more likely to realise any leadership potential.

> *I've recently noticed that often the female leaders in the world have been honoured and adored by their fathers.*
> *This includes the Asian region where women generally don't have a strong leadership role in the community e.g. Benazir Bhutto, the 'Persian Princess', Taj al Saltana, who started social work in Iran and others.*

Jacqueline Robinson – pharmacist, Perth

'Encouragement' versus 'Praise'

Encouragement is a better word than praise. Praise can produce a sense that they need to do things to please you, their father, rather than doing them for their own value.

> Rather than being a praiser, I am more of an 'encourager'.
>
> I don't want to create the impression that they have to do a certain thing in order to please Dad and get praise.
>
> I try to get them to work on pleasing themselves and monitoring their own efforts.
>
> When praising, I tend to praise the person rather than the action.

Peter Prout – farmer, soldier, lecturer in Education, teacher, pastor, Subiaco

Teaching her to handle fair criticism

One of the benefits of fair and sensitive criticism is that the children are then ready for the real world, a world in which critical appraisal is common, sometimes delivered sensitively but most often not. Being able to handle that criticism positively and effect change leads to personal growth, but failure to handle it leads to bitterness.[32] Inflated praise does not prepare them for that.

They will have to learn to deal with the negativity and toughness of the real world, so prepare them for it.

> Society has gone too far to protect children from the knocks in life by never having anything go wrong or providing negative feedback.
>
> An example would be school reports where teachers are so concerned with offending the child or the parents the comments are always positive.

Zyron Krupenia – clinical psychologist, Perth[33]

We need to demonstrate a strong belief in our children that they can have a go at things, take responsibility for failures, solve their own problems and not blame others if things aren't perfect. If we build up that confidence they will not see themselves as victims if things do go wrong.

Teaching her to handle mistakes and failures

It is crucial to teach the children how to deal with failure and mistakes.

Better to have them lose the game and teach them how to lose graciously than to let them win all the time.

John Inverarity — school principal, cricket coach, Test cricketer, Perth and London

If our daughters don't fail, then they haven't tried hard enough and they will not learn. If everything you do in life succeeds, then you will have failed. You sometimes hear the false notion that failure and weakness are the same thing. They are not. Failure makes you stronger and lack of failure makes you weaker. Every successful person has received bruises along the way.

It is so sad to see children reflecting their parent's desire to win all the time, and so heart-warming to see kids enjoying themselves, trying hard, being unafraid to have a go and fail, with their parents smiling at them on the sidelines instead of shouting at them to win.

Schools sometimes fall into the trap of not allowing kids to experience failure. Indeed there is a trend amongst parents and schools to not allow kids to see any of their attempted failures, in case it erodes their self-esteem. Better to help them work through failures than to pretend they don't exist.

> *During a race at school I fell over. It was humiliating.*
>
> *I looked up at the stands towards my parents and there was my dad, who was a successful sportsman himself, smiling at me.*
>
> *As I looked at him he pointed to himself, then drew a big heart with his finger, then pointed to me......he was sending me a message saying 'I love you'.*

Shari Serjeant – student, City Beach

> *Good judgement comes from experience, and experience comes from bad judgement.*

Mark Edwards – cardiothoracic surgeon, Shelley

Children who watch the 'Idol' talent competitions on TV often see their peers receiving criticism and evaluation for the first time. Although some of it is unpleasantly handled for the sake of viewer ratings, the fact that you can be evaluated and not become worthless in the process is an important truth to learn.

Fear of failure can prevent children from trying new things and thus they will not be able to make progress. Another effect of this fear is that kids wait until the time is perfect before they do something.

Fear of failure can prevent children from trying new things and thus they will not be able to make progress

We tell our kids that 'there is never a perfect time, just a better time', so don't be afraid to go out and have a go even if things aren't perfect. We say 'if you wait for the perfect time to do something, you will never do anything'.

Another helpful thing to teach your daughter is that 'her biggest weakness can become her biggest strength'. You must have seen this in others – they start with a weakness and work on it until it becomes a strength, something that often puts them ahead of others. Such a reality provides optimism and encouragement. It can also generate frustration in the process.

As a child, Dad always gave me jobs to do.

He let me make mistakes so that I might learn.

I used to get angry and say to him "why didn't you tell me?"

Jane Perkins – daughter of Harry Perkins, company chairman, Chancellor, Curtin University, Claremont

If you react badly to her mistakes you can destroy her confidence (e.g. 'you stupid girl, don't you know what you are doing – you could get us all killed?'). How you handle her mistakes, if you teach her to drive a car, is a good test of these concepts.

I can remember experiencing that myself when I was about sixteen years old. My father had decided it was time to begin to teach me how to drive a car, beginning with reversing out of our driveway. He told me to let the clutch out gradually and push the accelerator to give some power then gently reverse into the street. I tentatively tried it but I did not push the accelerator hard enough so I stalled the car. Dad said,"Give it a bit more accelerator next time, son."

So I tried again. I pressed the accelerator down firmly and the car screeched backwards in reverse, gathered speed as it accelerated fast along the driveway, careered backwards across both lanes of the street (fortunately there were no cars passing) and reversed up the long grassy hill on the other side of the street, finally stalling at the top of the hill on our neighbour's front lawn (fortunately they had no front fence).

I was a bit shocked and my heart was beating fast. The car was perched at an angle looking down the hill at the road below us. I was looking down, my knuckles blanched holding the steering wheel. My dad took it all in, then looked at me over his glasses and said, quietly, "Maybe a bit less accelerator next time, son."

It was a lovely piece of non-critical, non-judgemental fathering. I knew that I had done it badly and did not need him to shout at me and tell me the obvious. He was very accepting at the time. I guess that is why I remember it to this day.

If he had told me how stupid I was it would have crushed my spirit and more importantly, would have made me shaky the next time I tried to drive. But he was gentle, humorous and showed me he believed I could do better next time. I have never forgotten that moment.

Modelling

Modelling how we personally deal with our own struggles and failures is one of the best ways to help them develop the confidence to deal with theirs.

The reality is that irrespective of what you do every day, what matters a lot in fathering is how well you cope with tough times and how you model that for your children.

So worry about yourself when you're having a tough time, what words you use and how you go about handling it.

Dean Hirsch – President of World Vision International, Los Angeles

Encourage reasonable risk

We always let them take a few risks but did so within the protective family network.

We would not tell them what to do but would talk to them about it afterwards to help them work out whether they had made bad decisions.

Of course we did not allow them to take serious risks.

Geoff Marsh – Australian Test cricket vice-captain & coach, Perth

It is impossible to make progress in life without reasonable risk

Discussion of how mistakes and failures develop confidence requires a discussion about encouraging reasonable risk.

It is impossible to make progress in life without some risk. Although we yearn for a risk-free life for our daughters, the reality is that it is not possible. My daughter recently joined us in France after a backpacking trip. As she told us her travel stories I found myself bracing when I heard about the risk involved in some of them. But she is growing all the time as a person with these trips, so I know I need to encourage them. It is hard sometimes but as dads we have to allow them to take reasonable risks.

It seems to me that men stretch their children and give them encouragement to take risks, to move outside their comfort zone.

This risk-taking capacity seems to be more often given by fathers than by mothers.

It is incredibly valuable to children.

Geraldine Doogue – TV presenter, journalist, author, Sydney

Risk taking and failure requires dads to commit time with their daughters to discuss things afterwards.

Without some risk there is no adventure. Adventure not only provides opportunities to build confidence but adds an 'edge' that produces strong, rich memories.

Confidence building during discipline

It is easy, during times of discipline, to get angry and destroy confidence with phrases like 'you always do this', 'you never learn', 'you're hopeless', 'you've let your mother and me down yet again'.

> One low point occurred when we were driving home from Annapolis. My daughter Anna was pouring maple syrup into my youngest son's hair when he was about 3 years old.
>
>
>
> After about 5 demands that she stop, I pulled off the road, pulled her out of the car and spanked her, then put her back in the car.
>
> She was only 5 or 6 years of age.
>
> I always felt that I overreacted in that situation.
>
> I didn't need to be an overpowering dad.
>
> I had no right to do that - I could have responded 100 different ways.

Mike Lotze – surgeon and scientist, Pittsburgh

Instead of using confidence-eroding words or just overpowering her, show her you believe in her when you discipline her by saying things like 'this isn't like you' or 'you're better than that'.

If in the end you simply overpower her, how can she help but feel powerless?

Confidence building by service of others

When a child sees an image of a starving child on the TV news, she can feel helpless. If she can do something small to help, such as give some money or write to a politician, she can gain confidence that she is not powerless in this world. Serving others can make children feel more confident in life and have more control of their lives.[34] Being passive can create a feeling of helplessness whereas the process of taking action can induce a confidence that they can help the situation. They don't have to expect to change the world, just to do something. I love the old Chinese proverb, 'Better to light a candle than to curse the darkness'.[35]

Helping just one person can provide a profound experience of specialness and meaning.

Another benefit is that it distracts the mind from the little things of life – from 'the small goldfish bowl', and from one's self, i.e. it makes the child less ego-centric.

Fathers and father-figures are well placed to help develop this sense in a child. Some simple suggestions for service might include:

- sponsoring a child in a poor country (e.g. with World Vision)
- volunteering to serve in a soup kitchen (e.g. with the Salvation Army or Red Cross)
- raising money for worthy causes (e.g. with Oxfam-CAA)
- joining a community service group (e.g. Apex)
- writing letters to politicians about key issues
- working to help someone you know who is disadvantaged (e.g. doing the shopping for the elderly)

Exposure to the world of needs in a way that generates a feeling of being active rather than helpless can have a lifelong effect. I remember clearly how I felt different about my life after seeing how doctors and nurses helped destitute people during a medical student elective term I undertook in Nepal, a very beautiful but very poor country. That feeling has never left me.

In order to teach children about service, you do need to role model it. Sir Edmund Hillary did that with his children. After climbing Mount Everest, the first to do so, he raised funds to help build schools, hospitals and roads for the Sherpa people in eastern Nepal. He took his family with him to help, and in the process achieved a family bonding experience, a love of hiking in his kids and was a role model of service to the poor.

Dad had a desire to involve the whole family in the adventure of trekking into the Himalayas together and helping with the finishing touches to a small school or hospital. Those shared activities are unquestionably some of the best memories I have.

I think as a child one of the best things is to feel you are on a mission with the whole family; you are going to tackle this challenge together.

Peter Hillary – mountaineer,
son of Mt Everest pioneer Sir Edmund Hillary, Auckland

Confidence building by genuinely involving her in your decisions

Most of the dads I spoke to had never involved their kids in their major decisions in life. Those who said they had done so had either sat them down and informed them of their decision or pretended to ask for their kids' advice without ever really listening to it. Kids can spot that. To genuinely ask for a child's opinion in such important and personal circumstances is a great confidence builder. This is especially so for daughters and their dads.

> When I was about eleven, I recall Dad knocking on my door and announcing that he needed to discuss something with me. He was in the process of deciding whether or not he should seek preselection for the seat of Griffith. He made it clear that he was asking me not just because he knew the decision would impact on me and our family life, but also because he wanted to know what I thought. That meant a lot to me then, and it still does.

It is not an uncommon scene in our family for Dad and I to be on the veranda sharing a cup of tea and each other's counsel. I think, aside from playful banter and serious nurture, this is what distinguishes our relationship.

A father's respect for his daughter is invaluable.

Armed with the confidence that I am valued for my head and my heart, I feel ready to face life's challenges every day.

Jessica Rudd – daughter of Kevin Rudd, Prime Minister of Australia

Summary
Building up a daughter's confidence

- avoid sarcasm
- use encouragement
- don't use false praise
- during discipline, tell her you believe in her e.g. 'you're better than that'
- make criticism fair and sensitive
- help her work out her own plans
- model and encourage serving others
- invite her to help you fix things

Girls and confidence
– some extra things to think about

Adult daughters

- are you a confident woman?
- think back to the messages you received from your father
- ask yourself if you might be underachieving

Husbands

- ask yourself if your partner lacks confidence
- aim to help build it up rather than getting frustrated
- encourage her to have a go at new things, to make mistakes and to step out of her comfort zone
- to help your daughter to be confident, treat her mother as a capable person

Father-figures

- ask yourself if there are young girls in your life that you could encourage to believe in themselves more and to achieve their full potential
- encourage them
- tell them you believe in them

HONEY, I LOVE THAT YOU HAVE THE CONFIDENCE TO RUN FOR THE LOCAL COUNCIL ELECTIONS AS AN INDEPENDENT AND THAT YOU DELIVERED "HOW TO VOTE" PAMPHLETS AROUND THE SUBURB AND THAT YOU RANG THE TV STATION AND THEY'RE SENDING A NEWS TEAM OUT HERE...

BUT I WISH YOU HAD ASKED ME FIRST...

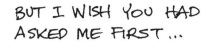

DADDY, I'M KIND OF BUSY RIGHT NOW... CAN WE TALK ABOUT THIS LATER?

Quiz Question

Who said: "If you have no confidence in self, you are twice defeated in the race of life. With confidence, you have won even before you have started."?

Answer: Marcus Tullius Cicero – Ancient Roman scholar, 106–43 BC

" One Christmas my daughter rang me and told me about the drugs she was taking.

When I was young I was into the full-on biker lifestyle. Lots of drinking, drugs, fighting, travelling around etc. All that stuff really.

I felt I could not chastise or advise her about what she was telling me without being outright hypocritical.

I simply heard her and let her know that I was here when she needed me.

Peter deBlanc – soldier, biker, IT consultant, Wembley

Chapter 5

Helping her say 'NO' to drugs and negative peer pressure

"Every dad has a lurking fear that his daughter might try drugs"

CHAPTER TOPICS

- Why drugs and alcohol are such a big issue for kids
- Confidence to say 'no' to drug taking
- Responsible alcohol consumption
- Strategies to avoid negative peer pressure

Why drugs and alcohol are such a big issue for kids

There is one area of life that I know most fathers are afraid of and want to protect their daughters from – substance abuse. Every dad I have spoken to has a fear of his daughter ending up on drugs. It is not just the disabling addiction, but for girls it is the increased incidence of risky sex, mental illness, suicide, chronic hepatitis, AIDS and prostitution, all of which are closely linked to drugs.[1] Girls with a strong relationship with their fathers are less likely to become drug addicts.[2,3]

It is easy for fathers and father-figures to get fearful for their teenage girls when they hear about the statistics on drug and alcohol use. It is frighteningly common in adolescents. For example in Australia, the UK and the USA between 20 and 60% of teenagers have used illicit drugs[4-7] and most have used alcohol.[8]

> *Drugs are every parent's biggest worry.*
>
> *When I was a kid parents would say 'I hope he never has to go to war' but now it is 'I hope he never gets into drugs'.*
>
> *Millions of parents out there would do anything to guarantee that their kids won't do drugs.*

Rod Marsh - Australian Test cricketer, English Cricket Academy coach, London

Some dads put their heads in the sand and think that it could never happen to them. But avoidance doesn't help - dads must get involved in talking with their daughters about substance abuse. The only way to reduce the chance of your daughter using drugs is to get involved. If you do you will increase your child's confidence to say 'no' and her resilience. You are potentially a lot more powerful than the police, or the school, when it comes to drug prevention.

Some of the results our own university research through The Fathering Project has shown[9] are:

- 80% of drug prevention education done through schools is undertaken by mothers rather than fathers
- fathers don't know how to talk to kids about drugs – 70% don't talk to their kids regularly about drugs at all and 95% don't talk to them about peer pressure
- the majority of dads average only a few minutes a day talking with their teenagers about anything
- the biggest limiting factor is not teenagers' busyness, family commitments or TV, but father busyness
- if poor fathering could be improved by just a little it would save governments billions of dollars in health care costs and crime costs

What we do is always talk to the kids about drugs.

Sometimes the kids are targeted because of my fame. There is some pride in snaring the child with a famous father and they imagine there will be lots of money.

We talk to the kids about how it could wreck their lives.

Geoff Marsh – Australian Test cricket vice-captain and coach, Perth

This issue is important, including for fathers who have been drug users themselves in the past. Even if it makes you feel hypocritical because you did use drugs, you owe it to your daughter to talk to her about risks of damage and the ease with which experimentation can turn into disaster – and when you do discuss drugs with her, listen to her rather than preach at her. 'Good listening' is discussed in chapter 9.

What drugs might cause problems for girls?

There are many drugs of addiction and as a father or father-figure you should know a bit about each of them – *cannabis* compounds like marijuana, *opioids* like heroin and morphine, *designer drugs* like Ecstasy, *brain depressants* like benzodiazepines, *brain stimulants* like amphetamines and cocaine, *hallucinogens* like LSD, PCP and ketamine and *inhalants* like glue.[10-15]

Alcohol consumption

Alcohol is the number one drug of choice for many adolescents.[16] Teenage drinking is a major issue and girls are as likely as boys their age to drink alcohol.[17] A recent survey showed that 40% of teenagers reported drinking alcohol in the past month and 25% reported binge drinking in the 2 weeks prior to the survey.[18] Adolescents aged 12 to 14 believe that the positive benefits of drinking (feeling good, fitting in with peers) are more likely to occur than the negative effects of drinking (feeling sick, causing serious health problems).[19]

Teenagers at highest risk of having alcohol-related problems are those who start drinking young, e.g. before the age of 15, have problem-drinking parents, have a peer group of drinkers, behave antisocially and are difficult to control, have been victims of abuse or other major trauma, have behavioural problems, struggle at school without support, have distant, unsupportive or rejecting parents, or experience severe, unpredictable discipline.[20] So avoiding these behaviours as fathers will reduce these risks in our daughters.

Alcohol-related events are a major cause of death and disability among teens as well as accidental death, e.g. by traffic accidents or drowning.[21]

Teenage girls who drink alcohol are more likely to become sexually active younger, have sex more often and have unprotected sex than teens who do not drink.[22] They are also at higher risk of rape.[23]

Abuse of alcohol alters thinking and removes judgment and coping skills.[24] It can lead to irreversible brain damage, sexually transmitted diseases, guilt, pregnancy, depression and suicide.[25] And in one study, of all children between 12 and 17 who drank any alcohol in the previous year, 39% had at least one serious problem related to drinking and 8% reported psychological problems related to their drinking.[26] Of young adults aged 18 to 20 who drank heavily, 66% drove under the influence of alcohol in the previous year and 42% often drove or rode without wearing a seat belt.[27]

Talking to your teenage daughter about alcohol

Alcohol is attractive for teenagers. It can provide feelings of social confidence and competence, social inclusion, an identity, pleasure, stress relief, rites of passage activities and humorous events (which become the 'war stories' of teenage life).[28]

Fathers, and father-figures, your daughter will frequently be offered alcohol and the pressure to take it to excess is strong. You need to prepare your own mind for this and prepare her for it. She needs to know the risks. She needs to be prepared with useful things to say, ranging from a simple, 'No thanks', 'I've had enough thanks' or 'I would really love a glass of water or a Coke' through to 'Please don't continue to pressure me when I've said no - it is starting to get annoying/it is not funny anymore.'

If you suspect that regular alcohol excess is an issue for your daughter, you might need to consider professional help. There is a vast difference between experimenting with alcohol and using it regularly.

Accusing, blaming, shouting and expressing your rage,

frustration, anger or loss of respect for her do not help much. Empathy and listening are better, plus helpful strategies.

Teach them to respect themselves

Respecting yourself and your body are some of the key strategies to help a girl look at the issue of drugs and alcohol clearly.[28]

> To help kids avoid drugs the parents need to be strong examples for them. Also, they need to treat their kids with respect so the kids don't want to disrespect their own bodies.

Justin Langer – Australian Test cricketer, City Beach

Clues that a girl might have a drinking or drug problem

The symptoms that alcohol or drugs might be a problem in a girl include:

- excessive mood changes, sudden temper outbursts
- irritability
- loss of enthusiasm for her hobbies
- memory and concentration problems
- reluctance for you to meet her new friends
- no pride any more in her appearance
- excessive defensiveness or rebellion
- finding alcohol in a bedroom or backpack
- alcohol on her breath or slurred words
- saleable items going missing from the house
- reduced interest in school
- reduced school performance for no obvious reason
- bloodshot eyes

Maintaining a relationship with a girl who has drug or alcohol problems

It is especially difficult to maintain closeness with a girl who is experiencing problems with alcohol or drugs. That is a vulnerable time and a fracture in the father-daughter relationship at this time is not uncommon and can be devastating. It can cause her, or you, to withdraw in hurt. She will sense a loss of your affection.

When I was a teenager I rebelled. I became angry. I ended up on drugs, which is why I am in this rehabilitation clinic now.

My father didn't know what to do when I became an angry teenager. It just confused him.

He loved me but he didn't know what to do.

But I can tell you this.

If he had just tried, and hugged me, it would have made a big difference.

Monique O'Neill – house warden, Sydney

Whatever problems your daughter experiences, be there for her and keep trying to communicate. She needs to know that you will still love her unconditionally and will not withdraw your love for her just because her problem upsets you.

Here is a piece of crucial advice I would give to dads - you can never hug your daughter too much and she is never too old to be hugged, told she is special and told that she is loved.

Most of us got into drugs between the ages of around 13 and 15 - that seems to be a critical time of change and dads have to really make sure that they are there for their daughters in those years.

Margaret Cox – heroin rehabilitation program, Brisbane

If you can communicate messages to her of unconditional love and unrelenting support, rather than messages of abandonment, rage, withdrawal and criticism, and you don't leave her helpless in the world, you will give her the best possible chance of turning things around.

Remember too that if girls end up in trouble with drugs they can be the ones who distance themselves from their fathers.

A lot of drug addict kids like me feel terribly let down by their dads.
But the feeling is also one in reverse.
I felt I just wasn't good enough for my dad.

Pamela O'Hara – recovering addict, Joondalup

If your daughter has a substance abuse problem the main treatment strategies to be aware of are detoxification, professional counselling (including family), treatment programs, self-help groups, avoidance of high-risk situations and treatment for associated mental health disorders such as psychoses and depression.[30]

Also, get help for *yourself* as well as for a child with a substance abuse problem. Remember too that this problem will put a strain on your marriage[31] so work harder at getting out together on dates and talking, especially about other things than her addiction. Get couples counselling if necessary.

Strategies to help girls avoid negative peer pressure

Parents ought to always assume that detrimental influences are present in any kid's life - drugs, alcohol, free sex etc.
So the best thing is to tackle it head on and talk about it. It's amazing what we talk about with our child's friends.

What's amazing is that they do want to talk with us about these issues.

It is often the first time these friends have ever discussed these issues openly with any adult.

Dean Hirsch – International President, World Vision, Los Angeles

One of the best ways to help kids avoid drugs and risky alcohol use is to deal directly with the issue of negative peer pressure and not assume that they know how to handle it. That means thinking about peer pressure, talking to your kids about what that means for them and helping them work out strategies to resist it, so that they choose what things they really want to do, not what their peers want them to do.

Preparing her with strategies to avoid peer pressure works – a study of 1673 adolescents showed that when kids are taught drug and alcohol refusal techniques, especially girls, they are significantly less likely to become involved with drugs and alcohol.[32]

Be intentional and direct on issues of peer pressure rather than pretending it isn't a problem or avoiding it. Talk about peer issues directly because to not do so, even because of your own concerns or embarrassment, won't help prepare her for that pressure.

Form relationships with her peers - a positive relationship with teenager's friends has been shown to reduce their risks.[33] And include her peers in your discussions – they will appreciate it if it is done sensitively.

A short summary of ways to help kids avoid negative peer pressure include:

- talk directly about peer pressure – don't avoid it, hoping it will just go away
- teach them useful, non-accusatory phrases to use to cope with peer pressure, such as
  - 'no thanks, not tonight'
  - 'not right now, thanks'

- 'let's not do this'
- 'thanks, but I am not really interested'
- 'I'm not really into that stuff'
- don't threaten teenagers or nag too much
- avoid always talking about how bad their friends are
- invite their peers to your house and encourage positive friendships
- listen to them without lecturing
- ask teenagers about their music interests, friends, issues and struggles
- remember that not all peer pressure is negative – encourage positive peer influences
- a good relationship with your child is the best insurance against peer pressure

Strategies to help avoid drug addiction

- get involved in drug education for her
- obtain drug information for your kids
- model strong values
- model a drug-free life
- give her strategies to say 'no'
- help her feel she doesn't need drugs to be acceptable as a person
- listen to her adolescent problems and concerns

Quiz Question

Which actor said: "Drugs? Every one has a choice and I choose not to do drugs."?

Answer: Leonardo DiCaprio – American Actor, b. 1974

> When we go camping, we go for a walk every night and I talk to them about the universe, the wonders of nature, what's out there and the mysteries of life.
>
> I teach them respect for education, knowledge and discovery all the time.

Peter LeSouef – Professor of Paediatrics, Subiaco

Chapter 6

Helping a girl become interested in learning

"*A daughter's attitude to learning is strongly influenced by her father*"

CHAPTER TOPICS

- Why it is important for dads and father-figures to be involved in a girl's learning
- How to encourage a girl's interest in learning
- Stimulating curiosity and open-mindedness
- Teaching and discussing values and beliefs

Why it is important for dads and father-figures to be involved in a girl's learning

Failure to learn can possibly lead to unemployability and a life lacking in self-confidence. It is important to create an atmosphere of interest in and support of a child's learning and curiosity.

Kids today will enter a tough world where there are many applicants for every job and mum or dad won't be able to get them that job. The youth unemployment rates for Australia, the European Union and the USA are all around 15-20% [1-3] and there may be 20 applicants, sometimes hundreds, for each job.[4] Educational failure leading to unemployment puts our children at the mercy of the down side of unemployment, e.g. loss of self esteem, depression, income failure and long term loss of employability.[5]

A father or father-figure can stimulate a girl's interest in learning, whether that is learning at school or about life, people and values.[1,2] If she lacks interest in learning it could affect her chances of getting a job. A lack of curiosity and basic problem-solving skills could make life boring and render her reliant upon others in life.

Girls do better at school if they have a supportive father.[8-13] In a study of over 1500 families, girls with fathers who were engaged in their lives achieved higher levels of education.[14]

This does not just apply to talented children but to children with learning difficulties as well – they do better in their learning and attain higher achievement levels if fathers are involved in their learning.[25]

One-on-one teaching is almost always more effective than teaching that occurs in traditional classrooms. Therefore, even if you are working long hours, you will have many more hours to teach her one-on-one than her schoolteachers. This is probably true even if you don't live in the same house as her – her schoolteachers just don't have that much time for individual teaching.

Some tips for fathers and father-figures to encourage a girl's learning

Maintain a positive attitude to her school

- show her that you place a high value on her education
- value, respect and *thank* her teachers and the school
- don't condone disrespect for the buildings of the school
- attend events like orientation days and busy bees
- volunteer for canteen duties
- don't condone school bullying (girls can be bullies too!)
- encourage other dads at the school to become involved in activities

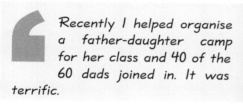

Recently I helped organise a father-daughter camp for her class and 40 of the 60 dads joined in. It was terrific.

Rocky Zamin – company director, Cottesloe

Maintain a positive attitude to her learning

- focus on her attitude to learning, and the progress she is making, not just results
- don't compare her to other girls
- if she is not academically gifted, show her you believe in her; she will be talented in something and you can find out what that is and encourage her accordingly
- appreciate that there are different intelligences[4] and acknowledge her intelligence(s)
- overcome the inner urge to see your children as potentially fulfilling your needs for affirmation
- remember that she is not studying just to become *your* ticket to 'bragging rights'

Be willing to help her learn
- help her with her homework
- help her set regular homework periods
- assist her when she is struggling
- help her develop good study habits - don't just nag
  (a list of helpful study habits is included on the book's website)

Stimulating her curiosity

I often hear complaints from parents that their children seem bored and lack any curiosity. Developing curiosity is not the same as doing schoolwork and learning facts. Kids can learn facts at school without being particularly curious.

Part of this lack of curiosity relates to modern culture where our children seem to be given little encouragement in life to develop curiosity. Children need freedom and encouragement to develop curiosity.

Kids are naturally curious and you have to be careful not to squash that. You've got to learn to draw their thoughts out.

The key is to not have all the answers but to stimulate questions.

Gay Crooks – paediatric cancer specialist & scientist,
Los Angeles

Fathers and father-figures can really help stimulate a girl's curiosity, even just by the way they play with her.[11-13]

Some specific tips to stimulate curiosity

Some things to do
- take her to the museum
- take her to the local community library
- help her to become interested in nature, world events and interesting people

- help her with school projects
- help her think 'out of the box' with those projects
- involve her in what you are reading, watching or doing
- explore the internet with her
- encourage reading, e.g. 'FART time' = 'Family Altogether Reading Time'

Some things not to do
- don't over-organise her life
- don't just complain about lack of curiosity, take her on 'journeys of curiosity' with you
- don't let her watch unrestricted television – it limits imagination

Responding during everyday life
- encourage imagination
- stimulate new ways of thinking whilst travelling, watching the news or performing tasks
- don't provide the answers to questions but encourage her to find the answers
- direct her to the place where answers might be found
- encourage open-mindedness and life-long learning
- teach her to question dogmatic statements
- teach her how to be a problem solver

Learning about values and beliefs

Our values in life (such as honesty, community service) are different from what we believe (e.g. Christianity, atheism, Islam) but together they provide us with most of our sense of meaning and confidence in life.[19-21]

Values and beliefs are generally 'taught and caught' from adults, especially parents. Fathers and father-figures are some of the strongest voices in establishing values and beliefs.[22]

> Fathers and father-figures are some of the strongest voices in establishing values and beliefs

Values

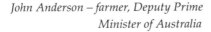
It's okay to push your world view on the kids - there are so many competing views out there and everyone is pushing their world views strongly so you've got to get in there and have the first shot.

John Anderson – farmer, Deputy Prime Minister of Australia

Having a solid set of values is a great foundation in life – kids who do not have them are often a bit lost, drifting around in a sea without solid islands as reference points.

There is ample evidence that the media has a powerful effect on children's values and attitudes, particularly adolescents.[23] But it has also been shown that parents can be powerful modulators of the effects of media, even by something as simple as sitting and watching the media with children.[23]

Fathers are strong influencers of values.[22] For example, fathers can be effective at balancing the media portrayal of gender roles, racism, attitudes to the poor, performance-driven and novel first encounter sex,[24,25] and the peer reinforcement of such values.[26]   And we need to be intentional about trying to balance those forces.

If you want your daughter to have strong values such as honesty, kindness, care for the helpless, integrity and compassion you will have to choose to be involved in teaching her those values. Don't assume that the school will teach values to your children. Lack of values can lead to unfulfilling and risky behaviour and, in its worst form, to crime and jail.

Parents need to share the responsibility of helping teach social values and morality.

You can't abdicate your responsibility and expect schoolteachers to do it all.

Kuan Tang – nurse, Leederville

Here are some tips on teaching <u>values</u>:

- be *specific* about values like trust, honesty, integrity, respect and racism
- don't rely on TV, movies, internet, magazines or peers to teach her values
- be generous and kind yourself to those in need
- teach them to accept people who are different, e.g. kids who are disabled, obese or 'uncool'
- develop their conscience about issues like bullying and abusers
- don't leave them in a 'values vacuum'
- look for incidental, teachable moments

If the other person isn't laughing then it isn't funny.

Dorothy Tribe – teacher, Nedlands

An example of how values are powerfully taught by modelling comes from my late father. A key example of this is not one of his higher profile community activities but a project he started 'to get kids off the streets'.

He formed a committee of young people from our working class neighbourhood to run a dance in a local community hall and to learn responsibility and leadership skills. It was a great success. It epitomised my dad's desire to undertake community service to help young people.

One night a carload of drunken young men tried to force their way into the dance hall. They tried to pull Dad outside to beat him up but he put his hands on each side of the door and dug his heels in. They tore his shirt to pieces. My sister was screaming.

He was not a churchgoer and had some problems in life at times with alcohol, illness and depression. I am intrigued to think of where his values came from. But he certainly modelled plenty of strong values for his three children. I probably wouldn't be writing this book but for him and I thank him for his example.

Beliefs

Beliefs, can be a touchy subject and I do not wish to offend anyone. But we do need to discuss beliefs with our kids because a) beliefs are important components of all aspects of society such as law, social services, moral values and education[27] and b) beliefs can have either positive or negative effects on life.

We all believe in something (atheism is a belief too), and our beliefs determine what we personally think is the nature and purpose of life and what we think is right or wrong. This is sometimes referred to as the 'spirituality' that we all have. We therefore shouldn't leave a vacuum in our kids' thinking when it comes to belief.

Beliefs in children have been shown to be powerfully influenced by fathers,[28-30] including the interpretation of media portrayals of beliefs.[31] Fathers can also turn kids off belief systems altogether.[32]

> **Beliefs in children have been shown to be powerfully influenced by fathers**

Failure to discuss beliefs and religion can leave kids feeling like they have been let down.

> My father rejected his Catholicism and remained indifferent to spiritual things and I ended up the same.
>
> There are times when I should have sought spiritual insight, but it never crossed my mind. I think I missed out and I think also that I missed out on developing that part of my own child's thinking.
>
> Fathers should encourage their children to develop their own spirituality. If not, it leaves a void. They should encourage them to at least think about it.

Jimmy Hart – US marine, Gulf War veteran, New York

A strong belief system can be a platform for early life. Kids might change their views as they mature, but a foundation is important.

> Children need a platform of spirituality in their life. They can then grow from that platform and develop their own spirituality, their own beliefs and values in their own time.
>
> But without that platform it is really hard for them - they don't have anything to build on.

Keith McAdam – tropical medicine researcher, Kampala

As with values, young children will tend to pick up aspects of their parents own particular belief system. Atheists tend to beget atheists, Baptists beget Baptists and Hindus beget Hindus.

This doesn't always happen, but most commonly it occurs because parents are powerful forces in shaping a child's early beliefs. And children's opinions will be strongly influenced by what you say and how you live out your beliefs.

> I am an atheist, although recently Tim has challenged me on that - he thinks my position should be agnostic.
>
> I guess I've passed that atheism on to the kids a bit because kids always tend to follow their parent's beliefs.

Peter LeSouef – Professor of Paediatrics, Subiaco

> *I used to go hunting with my father. We always talked on those trips.*
>
> *He was a different man out there when we hunted. There was a closeness, a oneness and a comradeship that wasn't quite the same at home.*
>
> *These experiences were so powerful that it made me want to be like him.*
>
> *I wanted his thoughts to be mine, his values to be mine and his God to be mine.*

James Dobson – psychologist, author, founder of Focus on the Family, Colorado Springs

Potential <u>positive</u> effects of faith in families

Religion in a family can have measurable positive outcomes. There are beneficial effects of a religious culture on girls, both because of the values taught and the close community in which they are taught and feel they belong. A study of 30 000 girls demonstrated that if they are in religious environments they have reduced risk of suicide, delinquency, drugs and risky sexual activity.[33] Of course these beneficial effects are found in several religious traditions and therefore they cannot define those religions as being true, just as being helpful. A lot of those benefits are derived from the promotion of strong values and a lot from the believing community.

> *When we lived in Philadelphia we had a lot of exposure to Jewish communities and we noticed how cohesive that type of community was for families.*
>
> *We are not Jewish, so we decided to attend an Anglican Church in Philadelphia and this for a while did provide just the sort of community that our children needed.*

Peter Doherty – Nobel Laureate, Memphis and Melbourne

Understanding the potential effects of religion on families is relevant to those with and without a faith. They are presented here so that the reader can be aware of them, ask if they apply to his or her life and avoid the negative ones.

Some of the potential positive effects of beliefs in a family can be:

- a strong community to share the load of bringing up children and providing a sense of belonging
- a practised openness to admitting mistakes ('confession')
- a practised openness to change ('repentance')
- exposure to lots of educational information and workshops on relationships and family life
- strong values and morality passed on to daughters
- a sense of purpose in life
- frequent reminders about the importance of unconditional love and specialness
- servant leadership, rather than authoritarian leadership, by fathers
- marriage enrichment opportunities
- the potential to use God as a role model of a loving father, especially in the absence of any other role model

 I had no strong father role models myself so I learnt by reading the Bible to find out what was required of me.

I learnt about what a loving father is by learning about God's character, particularly his unconditional love for me.

Harley Hayward – Aboriginal pastor, Balga

This is only a *potential* list - not all beliefs embrace all of these things, especially unconditional love, specialness and servanthood.

Potential <u>negative</u> things about faith in families

Religion in a family can also produce negative effects on children, ranging from excessive guilt to racism. It all depends upon what is taught and how that is worked out in the life of that family.

Some of those negative effects could be:

- oppressive rules of behaviour that can induce rebellion
- a heavy burden of expectation that restricts the personal freedom of children to grow into responsible individuals
- use of religious laws to discipline children, which can induce excessive guilt and fear
- inappropriate use of faith as an avoidance strategy by fathers and father-figures (e.g. having faith that God will protect a girl from absent fathering instead of just spending time with her)
- dogmatism and fanaticism that can be absorbed by daughters
- using God as an excuse to be a judgemental, policeman-type father or father-figure
- excessive focus on trivial issues
- restricted roles for women in some situations
- a closed community, which makes kids scared of the 'real world' and vulnerable when they enter it
- rigid feelings of authoritative certainty producing inflexible fathering
- an unnecessary fear of psychology and science
- absentee fathers who are busy working for a 'higher calling'

This is a difficult subject for me to write about. I was too busy preaching all over the world. Only Ruth and the children can tell what those extended times of separation meant to them.

I missed so much by not being home to see the children grow and develop.

Billy Graham – Evangelist[34]

 He was our daddy. I was glad to let him go. We knew he was working for God.

But we were raised by a single parent.

When your daddy spends more time with his secretary or reporters than he does with you, that hurts.

Ann Graham Lotz – daughter of Billy Graham[35]

My approach

I am a scientist who is trained to always examine the evidence and arguments with an open mind. This creates a conflict in my mind and possibly in yours, when it comes to what we want our children to believe. I know many parents who agonise over their children's beliefs, and how to influence those beliefs.

Because it is easier for kids to rebel against dogmatic parental views than against rational, fair arguments from an open-minded parent, I encourage my kids to think things through for

> It is easier for kids to rebel against dogmatic parental views than against rational, fair arguments

themselves. For example my son Simon once asked me, when he was about eight years old, "Dad, our school is going to hear the Dalai Lama speak today. Is he on our side,

Dad?" I told him that it was up to him to decide what he thought after he heard him speak, and that he had to make up his own mind about the Dalai Lama, and everything else, not have me make up his mind for him. I said I would talk to him afterwards about it. He pestered me about it but I kept telling him the same thing. And he has made up his own mind about what he thinks in life.

I think my own personal beliefs are built on a strong and defensible position that does not need to retreat behind a wall of dogma, so I have tried to talk with my children in a way that encourages them to not be afraid to examine other views for themselves. This is not a postmodern view that all other views are equally valid, it is an encouragement to examine all views with an open mind and decide which views they consider to be true.

This idea won't please some parents because it will create a fear that their children, having examined other ways of thinking, might choose one of them. But I think the opposite generally applies – many children of dogmatic parents have rejected utterly and permanently the belief system of their parents because those beliefs have been pushed on them without a rational basis and without them feeling that they have any real choice (i.e. 'believe, or else'). In contrast, where children see that their parents beliefs are based on a solid foundation and that their parents live out those beliefs congruently, and that their lives are enriched by it, it is harder to reject them.

I know that if I don't encourage my children to find things out for themselves they might either cling resolutely to dogma or spend their lives living in reaction to it, neither of which is healthy,

> Kids might either cling resolutely to dogma or spend their lives living in reaction to it

intellectually honest or a solid foundation for life.

That is just my approach and that of some of my friends, but I know others will have other approaches to this issue.

My own Christian faith has certainly helped me by exposing me to fathering information, helping me overcome my reluctance to admit my mistakes and to apologise for them. It has also exposed me to great dads who have become close friends and taught me how to be a better dad by words and actions. I would be dishonest if I did not acknowledge that. I hate to think where my personal drive and selfishness could otherwise have taken me.

But this discussion is not about a dad's beliefs, mine or yours, it is only really about our kids. I am suggesting that we ought not to encourage dogmatic views about religious beliefs, for or against them, but reasoned views based on evidence and rationality. That is a much stronger foundation for life than dogma.

Given that everyone believes something, we owe it to our children to help them to keep a genuine open mind in their search for what it is that they consider is true and thus worth believing in, regardless of what we think as their parents.

A daughter and her learning – some things to consider

Dads

- try spending at least one hour each week finding out what your daughter is learning about and encouraging her to find creative ways to learn new things
- help her develop good study habits – don't just nag (check the book's website for a list of tips)
- thank each of her teachers for teaching your daughter
- attend the next orientation day, canteen duty or busy bee
- take her to a museum or a nature walk
- reduce any over-organisation in her life
- discuss values and beliefs with her with an open mind after you have next watched TV together

Adult daughters

- how much was your attitude to learning new things and your level of curiosity influenced by your father?
- have you developed problem-solving abilities?
- did you learn your values 'at your fathers feet'?
- do you live in reaction to your parents' beliefs?
- encourage your husband to discuss learning, values and beliefs with his daughter

Husbands

- be aware of the effects of your wife's father on her sense of her own capacity to learn
- encourage your wife's curiosity
- respect your wife's ideas and beliefs
- consider how your wife's father has affected her values and beliefs, positively or negatively

Father-figures

- you are ideally placed to encourage a girl's learning – she will watch and listen to you
- sometimes you will be more effective than her own dad because you are an 'outsider'
- help stimulate a girl's curiosity
- work with her through problems to develop problem-solving skills
- encourage open mindedness to different values and beliefs

Quiz Question

Who said: "Live so that when your children think of fairness, caring and integrity, they think of you."?

> Fathers who have a close relationship with their daughters convey a strong set of values and commitment and this 'sets the bar high' for their daughters when they come to choose a life partner.
>
> I believe this has applied to my own daughter.

James Dobson – psychologist, author, founder of Focus on the Family, Colorado Springs

Chapter 7

Teaching her how she can expect to be treated by a man

"A daughter learns from her father how she can expect to be treated by men"

CHAPTER TOPICS

- Why girls learn from their dads how they should be treated
- 'Setting the bar' of respect
- Talking with daughters about sexuality and relationships
- Role modelling healthy conflict resolution and shared parenting

Why girls learn from their dads how they should be treated by men

A dad hopes that if his daughter marries, she will be happy, fulfilled and not suffer traumatic separation. He can influence that outcome.[1]

The relationship a girl has with her father has a profound effect on her subsequent relationships with men and especially on any marriage.[1] There is something about a young woman's relationship with her father that influences the way in which she looks for a male partner.

Many studies have shown that the father-daughter relationship profoundly affects a woman's subsequent male relationships, especially marriages.[2-11] Indeed the likelihood of a woman having a successful marriage relationship is strongly influenced by the relationship she had with her own father.[12-17]

This relationship can affect many aspects of a woman's choice of partner, her acceptance of disrespect, her sense of worth in the relationship and the importance she places on the values held by a man.[18] Poor father-daughter relationships can lead to fear of intimacy and sexual difficulties.[19]

The way a father treats a daughter determines how high she 'sets the bar' in male relationships

 I think the sense that you get about yourself from your father does influence who you choose as a life mate.

Bill also adores and cherishes me just like my father did, and he treats me wonderfully.

Bryn Freedman – author,
managing news editor, Los Angeles

Daughters 'set the bar' of how they expect to be treated by men largely according to how they are treated by their fathers.[20]

If her father has treated her badly she can assume that is all she can expect in life. Of course the reasons why daughters marry men like their fathers is more complex than that, but the notion of setting the bar at a certain height is its simplest expression.

There is no doubt that the relationship between a father and his daughter affects her marriage, for good or bad. She does not launch out into a long term relationship with a man entirely free of dad's influences.

I know that it is said that the relationship between a daughter and her father has a profound effect on her marriage and her confidence at work and I really believe that. It is certainly true.

The most important person in a girl's life is her father. He determines her confidence, her belief in herself & her relating to a man.

Philippa Mattick – scientist, Cincinatti

Bruce, I am having difficulties reading these interviews.

I mean no offence - they are interesting, but it is just that it reminds me of my own childhood.

I read them and I feel like cutting my wrists.

I'm crying now as I type them.

My father is a dentist and he was never there when I was a kid. We are close now, but not then.

I have had to have counselling about it.

They say 'show me how a girl relates to her father and I will show you how she will relate to men in her life'.

And that is true for me- my father's absence from my childhood has definitely created problems in my relationships with boyfriends.

Soo Lin Chan – typist, Adelaide

It is widely held that a girl's relationship with her father determines the level of respect she feels she deserves and the likelihood she will end up divorced or not.[1-6] It also profoundly affects her choice of marriage partner. The daughter of an abusive father or alcoholic is more likely to marry a man who is abusive or an alcoholic.[21-27]

The point is that a girl's father will end up affecting her marriage choices to some extent.

> If I'd had a good relationship with my father, it's hard to know how my life would have been different.
>
> I certainly suspect that I might have chosen my first two marriage partners differently.
>
> I was certainly looking for security, for the feeling of belonging and being cared for.
>
> Being able to depend on and trust someone else.
>
> I didn't get that in my first two marriages just like I didn't get it from my dad.

Yvonne de Blanc – social worker, Wembley

Dads, again, there is no opt-out clause to this. Treat your daughters well and you will set them up well for strong long-term relationships. Fail to show them respect, or worse, and you potentially set them on a course for disaster. You are not the only determinant of this - and there are no guarantees that being a good dad will protect a daughter from subsequent divorce, but you are a major determinant.

> A girl will not accept a man who is any less than her father is. That's why it's important for the father to create a good model for his girls.

Noni Reed – sole parents group, Cincinatti

Teach her to expect respect from men

Girls need to be treated with respect by their dads so they won't put up with any crap from some man who doesn't treat them with respect.

They will avoid those sorts of men in their lives.

Peta Fong – hairdresser, City Beach

A key word to emphasise is that wonderful word 'respect'. We discuss some of the components of respect elsewhere (e.g. listening to her opinions and respecting her private space). If she gets respect from her dad she will feel that she is worth respecting already. If a male shows her disrespect she will recognise it. She will feel she deserves better than that and, dads, you can help her expect that.

Because my dad respects me, I know what it is like to be respected as a person by a male, therefore I would not accept lack of respect from anyone.

I wouldn't form a relationship with anyone who didn't treat me with respect.

I am not sure if the person I marry will need to be better than my dad. I do know that my dad will question any prospective husband.

But in the end if he believes I love him then he will accept him.

Sarah Pocock – student, Milton Keynes

A daughter's sexuality - being willing to discuss it

Part of the process of influencing how a daughter relates to men is to be willing to discuss sexuality with her. Most dads find this a bit uncomfortable. But you have been a boy and have a boy's experience so she might listen to you if you talk about boys.

Fathers can have a positive influence on a daughter's sexuality. If fathers are not close and not involved, there is an increased risk of unhealthy sexual behaviour.[28-30]

There is some evidence that dads worry more about risky sexual behaviour (e.g. leading to pregnancy, sexually transmitted diseases, date rape and lasting guilt) than worrying about virginity per se.[31]

Some dads have told me that they think it is their responsibility to talk to their sons about sex but not to talk to their daughters about it – that is mum's job. I don't agree.

> There is some evidence that dads worry more about risky sexual behaviour than about virginity

Mum has never been a teenage boy herself so she needs help to explain how testosterone makes young men behave.

Dad should be involved in these discussions and in listening and talking with his daughter. If he does not she is at increased risk of becoming confused sexually.

If she says she is too embarrassed, tell her to 'humour you because as a dad you have to do it and would feel awful if you didn't, so could she just let you go ahead and tolerate it'. She will probably be really grateful in the end.

I remember taking my daughter Amy out for such a discussion. Because she and I had been joking about it, how it was something I had to do, she was 'ready'. We had a few laughs, but I was able to talk clearly about things like testosterone, respect and choices.

Fathers should talk to their daughters about boys. Don't leave it to the mother or to chance.

I remember when I was in ninth grade my dad was on a trip somewhere. He sat down on a plane and wrote me a 3-page letter about boys. He told me how it all worked, the positives and the negatives of relationships with boys.

He told me to always respect myself, to stand up for myself and to not allow myself to get into any situation where I might be 'talked about' by boys.

Danae Dobson – author, daughter of James Dobson, Pasadena

Helping her to understand males and dating

My father helped me think through things when my heart was broken, especially around the age of 20 when things seem more serious.

Dads can also help their daughters interpret the world of men.

Giovanna Lombardi – scientist, London and Rome

Help her understand what males are like and perhaps 'explain boys'. Talk about courtship and dating with her. Explain that no matter what they say when they are with you, boys like to talk about the 'adventures' they have had with particular girls.

I think daughters look to their fathers to answer the question "What is a man all about?"

They look to us to see how men think, feel, react and how well we take responsibilities.

They also learn the difference between men and women in terms of aggression, motivation, etc.

Peter Prout – farmer, soldier, lecturer in Education, teacher, pastor, Subiaco

I think that it is important to teach girls the difference between courtship and dating. When I was a young man at college dating was a bit of a sport and girls were treated as sport.

Courtship however means that girls learn to be friends with boys first, and because the secret of marriage is to have a friendship with your partner, this idea should make marriages more successful.

Todd Akin – Congressman, Missouri

Discuss sexuality values with her

Have you ever watched TV music videos? If not, stop next time and watch. Some of it is soft pornography. More importantly it promotes sexuality messages that could increase the risk that your daughter will have sex before she is ready. Then she is at risk of guilt and of sexually transmitted diseases, both of which are increased in girls who are pressurised into having sex before they are ready.[32] Watching TV together is also a good time to teach sexuality values.

Girls have a reduced likelihood of being involved in risky sexual practices when fathers intentionally discuss sex and talk about how to say 'no', are willing to talk about birth control if appropriate and talk about sexuality values.[33]

On TV kids see lots of sexual values which are fictitious, that would be a lousy foundation for real life.

I explain to them that this situation makes for a nice story but it doesn't work in real life.

To teach them about healthy lifestyle issues I find it more useful to comment on things that occur while we are watching TV rather than lecturing.

This is best done on the run such as after news items about drugs, TV shows about sexuality, TV shows with odd sexual behaviour etc.

Ian Robinson – desert tourer, pastor, Perth and Sydney

It is hard for her to make decisions about sex in a vacuum of information about values. This can be difficult because a lot of dads don't hold strong values about sex or if they do, they don't wish to push them onto their daughters. That means the values sold in magazines, movies, TV and the internet are unopposed.

There is a lot more sexual interaction going on than you probably realise – perhaps more than when you were young. A recent US study showed that teens are having oral sex in high numbers and view it very casually. More than half of the kids surveyed, age 15 to 19, had already had oral sex according to the US National Center for Health Statistics and the National Campaign to Prevent Teen Pregnancy.[34] And 87% of more than 2500 university and college students polled across Canada admitted to having virtual sex ('cyber sex') over Instant Messenger, web cams, or the telephone.[35]

A 2006 study of 745 adolescents aged 13 to 18 showed that 40% of the girls had been exposed to online sexually explicit material in the previous 6 months.[36]

Some indication of the number of teenagers having risky sexual intercourse is the recent publication from the Centre for Disease Control and Prevention which found that more than 25% of teenagers studied had a sexually transmitted disease.[37]

Given that not all sexually active teenagers will have such diseases, you will appreciate what that says about the amount of sexual activity amongst teenagers.

I wish to make it clear that I am not trying to prescribe a moral behaviour on the reader or on daughters. That is none of my business. What I am saying is that as dads we can help them make positive decisions about their lives that are not due to peer pressure, pressure from boys or images from media so that they don't end up doing things they don't want to do, having sex before they have really thought about it, having risky sex, getting pregnant or suffering a sexually transmitted disease, then regretting it all later.

In a study of over 1000 adolescents, father involvement was shown to have a major role in reducing a girl's likelihood of having sex at an early age.[38]

Remember that this issue is not about your views and feelings but hers.

Sexuality and Respect

The best strategies to help girls negotiate the world of sexual values involve the word 'respect', which we discussed earlier. Fear tactics like 'you might get pregnant or diseased' are not the best alternative.

> The best strategies to help girls negotiate the world of sexual values involve the word 'respect'

Respect includes *respect for yourself* - 'I don't need to have sex with you to be an acceptable person: I already am'.

It also involves respect for your body - 'my sexuality is

precious and I don't plan to give it away to just anyone who asks, especially a boy who insists on it'.

Respect for others is also involved, such as respect for parents. It involves *respect for any future partner* who will have to deal with the decisions you made about sex before you met him.

Of course this is made harder by the tendency for young people to think that the person they are with is the person they will be with for life, a common theme in the songs they listen to ('I will love you forever'). It takes a while to realise that he is not. Whilst that may or may not cause problems, the point is that she should know that any decisions she makes now may have consequences over time.

Young people think mostly 'in the moment' but also carry romantic notions about a happy marriage in the future so it could help to remind them that some potential future partner will have to deal with their current decisions.

I don't wish to suggest a heavy guilt burden be laid upon your daughter, but I am just suggesting that you encourage her to make her own decisions thoughtfully and not because of peer or media pressure.

If the father gives strong signals to his daughter that she is something special and she should respect herself and not let herself be used by anybody, she is less likely to try such activities.

When I was a teenager one of my 14 year old friends tried everything. She said to me once "sex is great". She was only 14.

But when I think about her back then I believe it's because her father never focused on her, never discovered who she really was as a person, so she was looking for that from other males.

Yvonne de Blanc – social worker, Wembley

Father-figures can also be effective in encouraging girls to respect themselves and reduce the risk of early casual sex if their advice is delivered carefully and appropriately.[39]

Teach her strategies that she can use to make her own choice

There are phrases that she can use without destroying her male relationships. She can say 'no' and generate healthy boundaries, and respect, without losing male affections. And if she does lose a relationship with an egocentric male, he was not the male for her.

There is no contraceptive for getting hurt
School sexual health advertisement

Prepare her for the usual things that boys say, such as:

- 'if you really loved me you would do it'
- 'everyone else is doing it'
- 'you know you want it'
- 'I won't date you any more if you don't'
- 'I have waited long enough'
- 'you're missing out on something wonderful'
- 'it's natural when you love someone'
- 'all of the other girls are doing it'

Give her words to use, probably with mum's help, for such times including times of potential sexual harassment. Make sure she knows it is OK to say 'no'.

Dads, don't leave it all to their mums, because you can have a powerful effect yourself.[40] If you are embarrassed to talk about these things, show her this chapter and ask her to read it, then talk to her about it.

Show interest in the sort of man she might end up with

A lot of the dads I spoke to did express some concern regarding the sort of person their daughter would marry, especially whether that person would love and respect her in the way she deserves to be loved and respected. If a daughter knows that her dad is concerned about this she will realise how important it is. Again, I am in no way suggesting that a father should interfere with his daughter's choices (he can't really have a major effect on her choices anyway), just show sufficient interest that she realises her dad cares about this aspect of her life.

> Dads do worry about who their kids are going to finish up with. You see kids who go and move in with their boyfriend or girlfriend, someone that they fancy but it's really a mistake.
>
> I guess the happiest thing for me as a dad is to know that my daughter's found a fantastic bloke. He is like another son.

Dennis Cometti – sports commentator, author, Perth

> My wedding day was very special when Dad 'gave me away'.
>
> I had a clear sense that Kevin needed to be - and that in Dad's opinion he was - worthy to marry me.
>
> I didn't feel that Kevin needed to be that worthy of me, but I had a clear sense that Dad did feel that.
>
> He wouldn't just give me away to anybody!

Rosemary Kendell – occupational therapist, Floreat

Searching for affirmation from a husband

A woman can be on the lookout for affirmation all the time from her husband in order to fill the gap left by her father. This is one of the problems that can arise in marriage as a consequence of the father-daughter relationship.[41-47] In that situation whatever affirmation a husband gives may never be enough. Then she can feel let down and he can feel helpless.

> When I was a young girl my father struggled with alcoholism and he wasn't able to give me the affirmation that I needed.
>
> Later in life, after I was married, I realised that this was still having an impact on me - I noticed that I sometimes found myself looking for all the affection and affirmation from my husband that my father hadn't given me.

Mary Mattick – teacher, Sydney

Sometimes daughters marry a man to 'heal' their dad

It is not uncommon for a daughter to go and marry someone like her father in order to 'fix' her dad or replace an absent dad by marriage.[48]

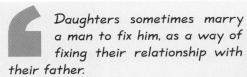
> Daughters sometimes marry a man to fix him, as a way of fixing their relationship with their father.
>
> Fathers should be the sort of man that they would like their daughters to marry because that is what will happen.

Jenesse Leung – lawyer, Toronto

How a father treats his daughter's mother will affect what she expects of men

Daughters watch how their fathers treat their mother.[49] This includes fathers who don't live with the family any more. So dads, bear that in mind. You are modelling, to some extent, how she will expect to be treated by any prospective future partner, so treat her mother with respect.

> *Daughters need to see their father treating their mother with respect because girls often marry a man who has some of the characteristics of their father.*
>
> *Given that little girls' first full on 'love affair' is with their dads, how their dads treat women are the first male characteristics that they notice.*

Jane Cookson — waitress, Melbourne

Model healthy resolution of differences in marriage

If a daughter sees you differ in opinion with her mother, but then resolve those differences positively, without recourse to harsh words or even worse, physical violence, she learns how to go about resolving conflicts well.

Modelling healthy resolution of conflict within a marriage positively alters a girl's view on marriage and her capacity to experience romance.[49]

> A daughter can learn how to resolve conflicts with men by watching her parents resolve them

To see no conflict creates a different problem because it creates an illusion that you are both happy together all the time. Your daughter might then be surprised when conflict occurs in her relationships – indeed because she has never seen conflict and certainly never seen it resolved maturely, she might automatically think that any conflict is a sign of relationship failure.

In contrast, if she sees your differences resolved she has a model to work with. Of course mum and dad might have major conflicts and it might take hard work to resolve them, but she will be watching and learning.

> *Once when I was really over-committed and had been away for 6 weekends in a row, I arrived home stressed and exhausted. Because I finally had a weekend at home I was so tired I couldn't talk and just wanted to do nothing.*
>
> *At breakfast the next morning my wife 'stepped on a land mine' by asking me to clean an umbrella because she had some people coming over.*
>
> *Our emotions collided and we got very angry with each other.*
>
> *We didn't talk to each other all weekend.*
>
> *But we had breakfast together on Monday morning and talked it through.*

*James Dobson – psychologist, author,
founder of Focus on the Family, Colorado Springs*

Father-figures are well placed to do this also. If a girl only sees unresolved conflict between her parents, a father-figure can provide an alternative example which might stay in her mind as a model. Some women I have spoken to had no role model at all amongst all of their family members and friends. A girl who sees a good model of marriage is more likely to end up in one herself - good relationships beget good relationships.[50]

> **Good relationships beget good relationships**

Model shared domestic roles

> My dad was a cop and a pretty conventional sort of bloke but he wasn't the aggressive, macho cliche.
>
> He was a shiftworker. Tried to do what he could around the house.
>
> Scandalised his siblings, I think, by helping mum with the laundry and the washing up after dinner.
>
> My mates found it interesting to see a copper in his singlet, ironing in front of the TV. You know, the handcuffs hanging off the belt.
>
> Geez, I thought it was normal.

Tim Winton – author, Miles Franklin awardee,
twice shortlisted for the Booker prize, Fremantle

Another way that a daughter's relationship with her father impacts on her marriage is the role that her father has taken in the house. If he has done nothing to help in the house she may more readily accept a partner who does nothing to help, even if she also works and comes home tired.

Helping with domestic duties, including child care, provides a helpful model to daughters.[51]

If she has had a father who helped in the house, cooked meals and embraced his role as a parent then she is less likely to accept someone who sits around expecting a woman to do all of these tasks.

" It is good for the children to see how their parents interact. Although I am a busy doctor I do most of the cooking so it is a role reversal from the traditional way of doing things.

Their mother is also a very successful scientist and doctor and it is important for both my son and my daughter to see that.

Michael Lill – haematologist, Head of Bone Marrow Transplantation, Cedar Sinai Hospital, Los Angeles

As with other aspects of modelling in marriage, father-figures are well placed to be alternative examples within the home.

Model shared parenting

" When the kids were young, Helen and I shared a lot of the parenting duties, changing nappies, bottle feeding etc.

We took turns at night to tend to the kids when they needed it. As they got older we loved snuggling up and reading to them before lights out.

Dennis Lillee – Australian Test cricketer, Claremont

If your daughter doesn't see her dad doing much of the parenting she might accept that her role as an adult is to do all the parenting too. Shared parenting has many obvious components, and some additional ones that not many men do. One of these things is looking after the kids to enable your wife to go away for a weekend or a week or month.

When I started doing this I was initially reluctant because I knew it would cut into my work time. But after I did it I realised how enjoyable it could be. Since then I have always loved doing it.

This has lots of benefits. One benefit is that you appreciate how hard mothers work at parenting. That's something I didn't ever fully appreciate myself until then. It especially helped me be sympathetic to sole-parents who do all the parenting themselves, without any help at all.

A second benefit is that you really have rich, fun times with the kids and become much closer to them.

In conclusion, girls learn a lot about whether they are worthy of respect or not from their dads. Given that, we as fathers, and father-figures, need to take that role seriously.

How a girl expects to be treated by a man – some extra things to think about

Adult daughters

- think about how your relationship with your father is affecting your marriage
- did you marry someone like your father?
- are you 'rescuing your father' via your husband?
- are you unreasonably expecting your partner to be like your father or replace him?

Husbands

- show respect for your wife
- don't take her for granted
- discuss what it was that she found attractive in you and what her expectations of a husband were and are
- role model for kids resolution of differences in marriage, domestic roles and shared parenting
- try to be understanding about her prior sexual history, especially if the issues discussed in this chapter are pertinent to her

---

Father-figures

- be ready to be alternative adults for teenage girls to confidentially and safely discuss their dreams for romance
- help them think through what sort of man they might like to end up living with
- remind girls that they are always worthy of respect
- listen a lot and give advice a little

DIANE WAS A PRACTICAL WOMAN. SHE KNEW SHE WAS LIKELY TO MARRY A MAN LIKE HER FATHER, SO SHE WENT STRAIGHT FOR THE MOST LIKELY CANDIDATE.

Quiz Question

Who said: "Don't worry that children never listen to you; worry that they are always watching you."?

Answer: Robert Fulghum – author, USA, b. 1931

"Dad, do you still love me when I am bad?"
That's what I was asked.

The number one priority in fathering is to make sure that kids know they are accepted regardless of their performance.

That is one of the keys. Our world is performance-driven. Kids will experience this at school, in sport, everything - only if you perform will you be accepted and liked. But no-one can live up to that ideal.

John Dickson – author, musician, pastor, Sydney

Chapter 8

Make certain she realises your love for her is unconditional

"She needs to know that her dad's love does not depend on her performance, looks or behaviour"

CHAPTER TOPICS

- Why unconditional love is vital
- What unconditional love means and doesn't mean
- The three ways to say 'I love you'
- Demonstrating your love for a daughter
- Speaking her 'love language'
- How father-figures can demonstrate unconditional love

Why unconditional love is vital

For a while I wasn't sure if Dad was on my side. That was during my teenage years. We clashed often.

I was rebelling about everything and he would complain about my short skirts, friends or long hair or stuff life that. He said he didn't want me to go out 'looking like a tart'.

But I always knew he loved me through all of this. I guess that was because he clearly showed me he loved me because he wanted to do things with me and enjoyed being with me.

Sandy Robinson – teacher, Bassendean

It is easy for the kids to think that they are only loved if they don't get into trouble, never rebel, do well at school or sport, if they are nice and never disagree. And even if they are truly loved unconditionally, it is easy for children to mistakenly think, during times of parental discipline or constructive criticism of academic results or other performance, that their parent's love is conditional upon that performance. It is vital that dads communicate this to their daughters. Failure to do so creates uncertainty and can make her feel unlovable or can make her strive to achieve things simply to get dad's praise. A perceived lack of this love from a father can lead to depressed mood, particularly in adolescent girls.[1]

True unconditional love is not commonly seen in families,[2] but when it happens it can produce 'breakthrough parenting'. This is when an authoritative parenting style, which can produce kids who are defensive and blame others, is replaced by a style of accepting each child and giving them freedom to grow and take responsibility.[3] One study found that true unconditional love provides a solid foundation for creativity, self-empowerment, self-confidence - the courage to step out and 'be who you are'.[4] Parents also gain from discovering unconditional love because it can help them modify their own attitudes and moods.[5]

> True unconditional love provides a solid foundation for creativity, self-empowerment, self-confidence

What unconditional love does not mean

What unconditional love doesn't mean is that the father becomes the daughter's 'pal', rather than her father. Sometimes a father permits any sort of behaviour and refuses to discipline his daughter because he thinks that might unsettle their relationship. This can be a trap for separated dads who want to show that they still really love their daughter.

Unconditional love means that she knows she is loved despite being disciplined. In fact it is kids whose parents let them do whatever they like who don't necessarily feel loved.

And unconditional love does not mean 'as long as you love your kids nothing else matters'. We heard that from John Lennon ('All you need is love') - kids need more than that. Love, by itself, is not enough. To better understand unconditional love, ask yourself who in this world loves *you* unconditionally? Do your friends and family show that sort of love for you?

What unconditional love means

I suspect that we all struggle to grasp what unconditional love *really* means. Unconditional love is hard to define. It has not been discussed much in the published literature, and this deficiency has been noted by others.[4]

> To better understand unconditional love, ask yourself who in this world loves you unconditionally?

Unconditional love means that our love for our daughter does not depend upon what music she likes, the friends she chooses to spend time with, her behaviour, her performance at school and sport nor her beliefs. As I listen to fathers disciplining their children or even just encouraging them to do their best, I can see how confusing it can get.

It can be relatively easy to say to one's children that you love and support them no matter what they choose to do. But it can be quite difficult to make it clear to the children that when you encourage them to study hard, your love is not conditional on academic achievement. The same thing applies to music, sport, art and other areas in which we encourage our children.

Parents talk proudly of their children's academic achievements and sometimes this becomes an extension of their own ego.

> Unconditional love means that our love for her is not withdrawn if she upsets us with her music, friends, behaviour, school results or beliefs

As a man speaks glowingly of the success of a friend's daughter, his own daughter can think 'deep down I bet you really wish that *she* was your daughter, not me'.

The notion of unconditional love is not trivial – everyone needs it. For example many of the powerful, rich or famous people I have interviewed are uncertain if their friends like *them*, or just the reflected glory or other things they might receive from this association with them (i.e. if they lost their power, money or fame would the love of those friends still be there for them?). They can yearn for the simple life of uncomplicated love, plus friendship that is clearly genuine.

Father-figures might also think about how they can show unconditional love, especially if a girl's father is not expressing this sort of love to her.

Responding to her behaviour

During teenage years kids can become quite difficult, even obnoxious, due to hormones, a strong desire for individuation or the stresses and pressures of teenage life.[6] Dads, during those difficult years continue to communicate to your daughter that your love for her is unconditional, that it is permanent and strong *despite what she does*. Never use rejection as a tool during those times because it can cause major anxiety in your daughter.[7]

> I remember when I was nineteen years of age I announced to Mum and Dad that I'd had enough of being good. But instead of Dad being angry, reactionary or disinterested he said to me 'You know we will always be there for you and we will love you, no matter what you do'.
>
> If Dad had gotten upset and 'thrown a wobbly' I don't know how I would have reacted. Or he could have said nothing - that would have been much worse.

Pauline Dixon – social worker, Rosalie kindergarten

Responding to looks and personality

It can be difficult for fathers to give strong unconditional love signals when it comes to looks and personality, yet it is important. Girls who are attractive with sweet personalities receive a lot more positive feedback socially than girls who are not.[8]

And this starts early in life. It becomes very difficult for a young girl who is unattractive to believe that her father's love for her is not diminished by her lack of attractiveness. She may watch how differently her father reacts to her compared to her more attractive sister.

This also applies to her personality – a child with a difficult personality will be much harder to show love to than a child with an engaging personality. Again, her radar can be out to see whether her father's love is diminished by her personality.

Sometimes girls will misbehave deliberately in order to test their father's love or to 'prove' that they are indeed unlovable. I have seen that often, and you probably have too. Dad needs to continue to show unconditional love even when this happens.

It brings tears to my eyes when I hear adult women talk about how the love of a father, grandfather, stepfather or other father-figure was always there even though they weren't the prettiest or the nicest girl in the family.

Responding to her school performance

We live today in a society that is much more oriented towards academic performance then previous societies. Part of that is the changing nature of work and is quite reasonable – children no longer expect to be able to get a job automatically when they leave school.[9]

Some of these changes in employability are welcome – no longer is promotion about who you know or how long you have been in a job but is based on performance. But that does create a pressure at school to perform.

This feeling of the need to perform successfully is especially powerful for adolescents who are under great pressure academically and athletically to perform to a high level and in an acceptable style.[10-13]

Whilst we need to pay attention to their results because they are important, we must be careful to communicate that their results are not *them* and that our love does not depend upon those results.

> My father did have expectations of me. If I came home with a school result that was A minus, my dad would say "Did anyone get an A?"
>
> I felt his love was conditional on this performance. The end result though was that I could never have been happy just being a housewife - my father certainly would not have been happy if I'd just been a housewife.

Sharon Greenberg – occupational therapist, Seattle

Responding to unwelcome beliefs and attitudes

Another area that is sensitive to many fathers' hearts is the set of beliefs and values their daughters choose to hold. This is especially the case if the father holds deep religious convictions and his daughter chooses to reject them, or even believe in something that is the opposite to her father.

> In our family it is very hard to change beliefs. When I became a Christian my family treated me like a stranger. I was sad then and it still hurts, which is why I am crying now.

Betty – communications technician, Jakarta

Similarly, if a father holds strong views on politics or deep convictions on moral issues and his daughter strikes out on a different path, it is a challenge to let her know that although he disagrees with her views, there is nothing that could ever get in the way of his love for her.

Given all of that, it can be really hard to convince our daughters that our love for them is unconditional, especially for some girls. How can we convince them?

Keep showing love when it gets hard to do so

Unconditional love can be hardest to give when deception and lying occur (e.g. about what they are doing, their friends and where they are). This is common behaviour in kids with drug problems.[14] I have had mums and dads weeping to me about it in fear and frustration. It can gradually erode trust and poison your relationship with them.[15]

> *I became a very angry young woman around the age of 10 and by the age of 15 I'd left home and began doing hard drugs.*
>
> *I wrote a letter to my father - I was pretty messed up at the time, but he didn't like it and said it was a "crock of s**t". I guess because I was blaming them and everyone instead of taking responsibility.*
>
> *But that's how I felt at the time and I think it's really important for fathers to try to hear what you are saying, even though it doesn't make sense. They need to understand what kids are feeling.*
>
> *I realise now that my life is really my responsibility.*
>
> *But if he had just reached out to me and given me a hug instead of getting angry all the time I think I might not have ended up on drugs.*

Montana Coghlan – heroin rehabilitation program, Brisbane

We need to continue to beam out unconditional love, like a lighthouse, because kids with major problems often hold themselves in low regard and are often depressed.

If the lighthouse of unconditional love is turned off, how will they ever find their way home?

> **If the parental 'lighthouse' of unconditional love is turned off, how will they ever find their way home?**

Try to continue making them feel worthwhile and keep telling them that you believe in them and that they will get through this time. Continue to listen to them. Do special things with them so they know that they are worth spending time with.[15]

There is evidence that this works – a study of 302 adolescent girls showed that continuing to beam out love, rather than anger and alienation, leads to better long-term emotional well-being and less behavioural problems.[16]

<u>Show</u> her your love physically

There is something fundamentally doubt-destroying about showing love physically by touching and hugging appropriately.[17] Why does a child who has fallen over run to her father or mother for a hug even though she isn't really hurt? Because the receipt of physical affection is a deep need of humans. Showing a daughter love by physical affection gives a powerful signal that she is loved and that she is lovable.

I still hug my girls all the time.

Some of my fondest memories with my children, especially when they were young, were the times of close physical contact.

For example those times at the end of the day when they would fall asleep on my lap, or over my shoulder.

And I was happy because when that happened everything felt like it was alright.

Bill Bryson – award winning author, Norfolk

Appropriate touching from a father is important for a girl's development[18] and its withdrawal can have measurable negative consequences.[19]

Hugs overcome uncertainty about how you feel.

> *Fathers need to hug their daughters.*
> *I like hugs from my dad - I get quite a lot, every day.*

Sarah Pocock – student, Milton Keynes

The importance of showing love physically is supported by the views of children. For example here are some of the responses from children of our local kindergarten to the question 'How is your dad special?' Notice how many mention physical expression of love.

My dad is special because he kisses me and likes to cuddle me.

Anna

My dad is special because he loves me so much and we like to have cuddles and kisses.

Lucy

Father's Day notes from Rosalie Kindergarten children

My dad is special because:

- *my dad puts me on his shoulders so I get so, so high up in the sky, but not really up to the sky because the sky takes forever.* **Samuel**
- *he hugs me a lot.* **Amber**
- *he likes me and he kisses me and gives me hugs.* **Rachel**
- *he carries me and he is strong. He loves me.* **Rebecca**
- *he is soft and cuddly.* **Kate**
- *I like to run into his hands because he's the best dad in the world.* **Daniel G**
- *my dad likes to tickle me all the time and he laughs when he tries to tickle me.* **Tom K**
- *he picks me up and gives me a fireman carry.* **Lauren**
- *he tickles me a lot and gives me lots of hugs. He earns money to buy toys.* **Emma**

Showing love during tough transitional times

> I remember on a couple of occasions saying "I hate you" to Dad. He always immediately replied "Well I love you".

Mimi Packer – daughter of Harold Clough, Clough Engineering, Mosman Park

It especially important to show unconditional love and physical affection at times when your daughter is in difficult transitional stages in her life. Such times include going to a new school, attending high school, puberty and during any family break-up.[20]

At such times it can be hard for dad as well. His daughter might appear to be losing interest in him, rejecting him or she might even say she hates him. At a minimum he might feel that he has 'lost his girl'.

> When I was in junior high I found that I had a couple of years when I didn't open up to my parents and I withdrew and didn't hug them much. I had some difficulties, a new school and all the hormonal changes that affect your life and behaviour. It hadn't been Dad who had changed, it was me.
>
> There is a picture taken of our family at the time in Hawaii and my dad has his arm around my waist and I am clearly looking down at this hand as if to say 'why are you touching me?'
>
> It was just a phase and it passed.

Danae Dobson – author, daughter of James Dobson, Pasadena

At such times dad will have to make an effort to adjust to these changes and continue to 'be there' for his daughter and make sure she knows he still loves her.

When she becomes a teenager she really needs for you to continue to show love by what you say, and physically, even though it is a complicated and sometimes a tough time of change for her.

My dad was really good at showing affection.

Importantly he didn't retreat from showing that affection when I went through puberty.

Cailey Raffel – teacher, Shenton Park

At these times you might also consider trying to get to know the music *she* likes, take her out to places that *she* wants to go to, buy a magazine about one of her interests so you can learn more about it and take vacations that are interesting to her rather than just to you.

It is during these transitions that father-figures are so important, even if she has a close relationship with her natural father. Indeed if she is really close to her father then an alternative strong father-figure is important as she 'individuates' away from her own parents.

Understand her love language

One final point about unconditional love relates to the notion of finding out the way in which your daughter best experiences love.

I am grateful to Dr Gary Chapman for writing about the five love languages.[21] It is a useful way to think about showing love to someone in a way that makes them realise you are making an effort.

His idea is that there are five main ways of showing love and that for each of us, one of these ways is dominant. A man brings flowers home to his wife but she doesn't seem to respond, so he gets angry. It may be that receiving gifts is not her love language. Because he doesn't know that fact he gets upset. What he needs to do is to find out what her love language actually is, and to 'speak' that language to her.

Children have these love languages too so you need to think about which one is dominant for your daughter.

These five Love Languages are as follows:

Words of Affirmation: This means that your daughter values positive things you say about her. Statements such as 'you look so beautiful tonight' or 'your help in that was the key' are examples of words of affirmation. Words of encouragement and valuing a person's opinions are others.

Quality Time: This means focussing on your daughter, not just hanging around, watching TV or whatever. Quality conversation is an important component of this.

Receiving Gifts: For some people this is a great symbol of love but for others it doesn't matter much.

Acts of Service: This one surprised me when I heard about it but it turns out it is my wife's main love language. It's a good thing I found out about it so I didn't get frustrated when I did things that I thought should matter. If 'acts of service' is her main love language, help her with a task or do it for her as a spontaneous act of generosity. Remember, this is a language of love, not of obligation or a score-keeping exercise.

Physical Touch: This means the demonstration of physical affection. This is my own love language. Some kids feel most loved when they receive a hug or other appropriate touch.

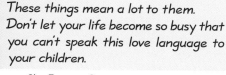

> *Daughters need love from their dads. Daughters also need to be appreciated for who they are. The little things that you do to show affection to your daughter are a love language that is special for each child.*
>
> *These things mean a lot to them. Don't let your life become so busy that you can't speak this love language to your children.*

Jim Ryun – Congressman, 800m, 1500m and mile world record holder, Kansas

Knowledge of the different love languages can transform relationships. Whilst everyone likes to have love communicated by all five languages at times, usually one of the five predominates. People tend to naturally assume, without thinking about it, that their own personal love language is the same love language as that of their partner or their kids.

> **Make an effort to find out your daughter's dominant 'love language' and to speak that language**

If you make assumptions about what your daughter's love language is you might not get it right.

What is your dominant love language? Understanding what it is and the love language of others puts you in a stronger position to communicate love better.

'Tough love'

Love is not always 'soft'. 'Tough love' includes a willingness to make certain that kids take responsibility for their actions and to not avoid discipline when it is required.[22]

Some dads have told me that they worry that showing lots of unconditional love and providing a safe and secure emotional environment will make their daughters soft, and that maybe the best thing is to 'toughen them up'.

Whilst it is true that kids who have lived tough lives quickly develop sophisticated ways of dealing with adult-type situations, they pay a price for that - they can become emotionally stunted in that process and have difficulty expressing and experiencing love. They can end up insecure and emotionally shut-off.[23]

Ironically, the more love and security a girl receives the less likely she is to become dependent and the more strongly independent she is likely to be.

<u>Tell</u> her you love her

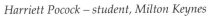

The most important thing a father needs to do for his daughter is to say I love you lots and to give his daughter cuddles every night.

Harriett Pocock – student, Milton Keynes

How do your children know that you love them? A number of the fathers that I interviewed were certain that their children knew that they loved them so they didn't need to actually say it. But many of their children actually described an uncertainty about whether that unspoken love was really there or not.

It was common amongst the adult daughters that I interviewed for them to be not quite sure whether their father had really loved them because he never said it.

So tell them and thus leave no doubt.

Sometimes it doesn't take many words to convince a daughter that you love her, especially if you are not a verbal person. So make the effort when opportunities arise.

She will always remember words spoken at any sensitive and important time.

But don't use empty, repetitive words.

But you've got to be careful - saying "I love you" can be a bit lazy, equivalent to saying "good morning".

You have to spell out the fact that you love your kids to them each time.

Ben Timmis – radiologist, London

I have talked to many groups about three different ways of saying 'I love you', and many have found it helpful.

You can say 'I love you' emphasising each word differently.

The first is 'I love you' (so 'you should be grateful', or, 'how could you do this to me when I love you so much?')

The second is 'I love you' ('can you feel my love - it is intense'). That is better, but it would stop if I died (i.e. it depends upon me). It is not a bad way of saying 'I love you' but not the best way.

The third way is to say 'I love you' ('you are lovable, worthy of love and others will love you too'). This is the best way, because it is most effective at making a child feel that they are indeed lovable.

> **The three different ways of saying I love you**
>
> I love you
> I **love** you
> I love **you**

Which of those 3 ways do you express your love for your daughter? I mistakenly used to stop at the second way ('I love you'), thinking that I was doing the best job I could as a dad by saying it that way. I am glad I saw that the third way of saying 'I love you' was more helpful to her.

It is from dads that daughters really need to hear this. Of course mums are important, but it is dads whose love kids are often most uncertain about. And if daughters don't have this clear statement of unconditional love from their dads, they can find it troublesome.

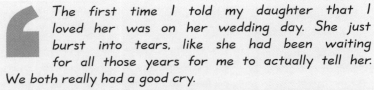

The first time I told my daughter that I loved her was on her wedding day. She just burst into tears, like she had been waiting for all those years for me to actually tell her. We both really had a good cry.

I think since that day it's just been something that's almost broken the ice. It's a lot easier now that I've actually done

it. Obviously I've taken a long time, too long, to tell her, but now it's happened it's one of the best things.

Graeme Smith – stonemason, Myaree

On my wedding day, when he did tell me he loved me, finally - because it only took him 25 years to do - it made me realise he had noticed that I was this living being in his life, that I did mean something to him.

I am very teary now thinking about that moment.

It was a very emotional moment, as it is now, just thinking back to that time.

Joanne Smith – daughter of Graeme, Coogee

In hindsight, I don't think I was very good at telling them, that I loved them. There weren't enough times.
If I could do it again I would tell them every day.

*Peter Prout – farmer, soldier, lecturer in Education,
teacher, pastor, Subiaco*

Unconditional love includes forgiveness

It is probably obvious, but needs to be explicitly stated here, that this sort of love includes the capacity to forgive. That doesn't mean condoning everything, but forgiving the person independent of the problem. Failure to do so can make the problem worse.

Last night I was talking to a drug addict. She was frightened that I would tell her dad about her drug habit.
Why?
Because she knows that her dad does not understand forgiveness and the important principle of talking and listening in relationships, about asking for forgiveness and receiving it.

George O'Neill – drug rehabilitation doctor,
researcher, obstetrician, Subiaco

And once forgiven, it needs to not be brought up again. Unconditional love is a scoreboard-free zone.

Unconditional love is a 'scoreboard-free zone'

Unconditional love means always 'being there' for you daughter

There is something special about a dad or father-figure always being on a girl's side. Kids learn from their earliest days in the playground that the world can be a tough place. They need to know that you are there for them when no-one else is.

The notion of being there for your children is one that I have found a lot of men don't think about. I was particularly struck by the need for children to know this when I heard a lecture given by an adolescent suicide expert. This person described the reasons why teenagers commit suicide. He listed some of the things that are written in the suicide notes that these children leave behind.

One of those suicide note phrases that stuck in my mind was, "There is just no-one on my side". There are published studies on suicide risk in adolescents that make the same point.[24,25]

Make sure that your kids know for sure that you are on their side, not just 'on their case'.

Is there anything that your daughter could do that would cause you to remove your love from her? And when things do go wrong in her life, do you accept her but with the wrong attitude - we can 'be there' for her but in a grumpy, reluctant way. That is not unconditional love, but a stern, folded arms, judgemental and punitive 'being there'.

Kids need to know that whatever happens, we will love them. We mightn't like what has happened and we might feel angry, sad or bewildered, but they need to have a clear message that our love will never cease.

I tell my children that if they ever get involved in any criminal activities, have a teenage pregnancy, become drug addicts or prostitutes or anything at all, that they would always know that I would be there for them. They could come to me and I would have open arms and my love for them would continue unconditionally.

What happens if you don't show her unconditional love and affection?

> *A female with a close loving relationship with her father will search for someone like him to marry. A female who is rejected and has no father to affirm her beauty and worth will spend her life looking for someone to replace the absent father.*
>
> *Of course this doesn't apply to every female, but the pattern is common.*

> James Dobson – *psychologist, author,
> founder of Focus on the Family, Colorado Springs*

Lack of *affection* from a father can have a similar effect to the lack of *affirmation* that I discussed earlier - she may look for that affection from other males, searching around for the love she feels she is missing.[26] Of course there are other reasons, but that one is the most common.

If a daughter doesn't get affection from the first male in her life, her father, she will look elsewhere. Indeed it has been shown, and reinforced by many social workers and psychologists, that one of the most common contributing factors to promiscuity in teenage girls is a search for the love and affection that their father did not give them.[27-32] Of course there are other reasons, but that one is the most common.

Using sex or any other strategy to get the affection that is missing from a father or father-figure is not a healthy basis for relationships and for sexuality.

> *Girls who don't have a sense of leadership and affection from their father are more likely to play around and become floozies.*

> Noni Strang – *sole parents group, Cincinatti*

> *I know that because I never had a sense of being loved, accepted and affirmed as a special person by my father I definitely fitted into that category of woman who was at risk of becoming sexually promiscuous.*

> Brenda Hodges – *teacher, Sydney*

Relating to boys is a normal expression of a girls individuation and separation from her father during teenage years and that is part of 'giving them wings' discussed earlier. I need to emphasise that I am only discussing unhealthy relationships with boys.

Girls who end up in prostitution talk about absent father love. Although it is often drug addictions that drive girls into prostitution, the lack of love from a father is another factor.[33]

> **If you don't hug your daughters enough, someone else will do it**

> I had a lousy father - he was an alcoholic and I never got the love I needed. After a couple of failed long-term relationships and some time overseas I returned to prostitution. I felt bad about myself but what else could I do.
>
> My mother loved me and treated me as being special, and she still does, but I know for sure that my life would have worked out very differently if I had also had a father who loved me.

Sarah Gisbers – prostitute, Sheffield

> It is crucial for fathers to show their daughters affection.
>
> If you don't hug your daughters enough, someone else will do it.

Todd Akin – congressman, Missouri

Showing continued love despite divorce

Separation is a time when a daughter can acutely feel that dad's love has diminished, that he is no longer there for her. Even though you don't live with the family any more, your daughter needs to know that you still love her and you will be there for her. This is discussed further in Chapter 12.

Showing unconditional love for a girl – some extra things to think about

Adult daughters

- were you loved by your dad, despite anything?
- did he have trouble expressing his love?
- thank your dad for any love shown
- encourage your husband to show unconditional love

Husbands

- think about whether your wife believes that your love for her is genuine and unconditional
- consider how much of any such feelings come from feeling uncertain about being loved/lovable by her father

Father-figures

- make sure you do not shower more attention on a granddaughter, niece, pupil etc who is fun, beautiful, mature, talented or well behaved than another who isn't
- maybe that 'black sheep' is the one that you can have the most positive influence on
- think about which girls you are in a position to communicate to that they are loved despite anything they do

Quiz Question

Who said: "To be brave is to love someone unconditionally, without expecting anything in return."?

Answer: Madonna – singer and actor, USA & UK, b.1958

 You must allow your children to always express themselves, even if it is painful to hear what they say.

You have to not be afraid to hear it.

Herb Stein – Emmy Award nominated director of
'Days of Our Lives', Los Angeles

Chapter 9

Become a better listener

"Daughters want their dads to listen to them more and preach to them less"

CHAPTER TOPICS

- Why listening is important to daughters
- How to improve your listening skills
- Some helpful things to say
- Some things <u>not</u> to say
- Dealing with emotions
- Listening to teenagers

Why listening is important to daughters

Poor listening is one of the biggest flaws that fathers have. At least that is what our kids say, especially our teenagers. Our Fathering Project research team has held seminars for community groups who work with young people. They report, almost unanimously, that the most common issue teenagers have with their parents is a *failure to listen to them.* Dads were the worst offenders.

A great way to show a girl that you love her and that she is worthwhile and special is to genuinely listen to her. Girls are often more verbal than boys so listening to them becomes really important. Failure to listen becomes a real risk for the relationship, leading to long term communication breakdown between a father and daughter.[1]

> Poor listening makes kids feel alone and anxious

Having a father or father-figure who listens is important for all kids, but especially adolescents.[2] Good listening builds self-confidence in children[3] and reduces their risk of depressive symptoms.[4,5]

Poor listening makes kids feel alone and anxious. A study of 1106 high school students showed that poor listening makes them feel alienated and puts them, particularly girls, at increased risk of anxiety during adolescence.[6]

Poor listening is common amongst dads

Most dads find genuine listening difficult – we either don't pay attention or we start preaching. If we don't listen it means the discussion becomes selfish on our part, whether we are giving our opinion about something or telling her how to think. A failure to listen can convey a failure to love.

> If I had my time all over again I would listen to the children much better.
> I've realised that trying to correct people all the time just destroys relationships in the short term and I don't want to do that.
> It's taken me a while to learn.

Ray Arthur – pig farmer, builder, pastor, Maddington

Fathers are typically less engaged listening to a daughter's emotional life than mothers,[7] and even then girls don't disclose everything to mum.[8]

It is ironic that sometimes the more a father loves his child the less likely he is to listen – it requires a lot of patience, intentionality and tongue-biting. The reason for this is that when children express opinions that on

> **Failing to listen is the most common complaint that teenagers have about their parents**

the face of it sound potentially dangerous, it is easy to have an anxiety attack and begin preaching (e.g. when they talk about taking drugs).

However, children feel loved when we listen to their opinions in a way that genuinely values them.

And good listening means that you get to ask about the other person. How often have you talked to someone you have just met at a party and after some time you realise that they haven't asked *you* anything about yourself at all, no matter how much interest in their lives you have shown? That is just what daughters often say about their dads.

Dad

Why do you insist on telling me what I'm thinking all the time? When you say that, it makes me want to run away from you.

You think you know me and understand me but you don't.

Why don't you ask questions before going off on one of your little speeches?

You don't like most of my friends, but at least they understand me. They listen, and they don't judge me. They just love me.

You say you love me every day, but if you really did you would try to understand me.

Jennifer – student[9]

Dad, how well do you know your daughter, her favourite musical group, favourite colour, the names of her friends, the magazine she reads and her biggest joys and fears? Maybe you could visit her bedroom and ask for a guided tour of the special photos and memorabilia she stores in there.

Why do we fail to really listen to our daughters?

It requires time to listen – time from dad and time from a daughter. Girls can get busy socially so be willing to make time, including fitting in around her timing and on her terms. This requires effort. Listening requires that we make that sacrifice of time when the opportunity arises.

One of the best talks I've had with my daughter occurred one night, a few years ago, when she'd been out very late. I think it was about 4.30am. I went downstairs to make a cup of tea and she came and she just started to talk. She talked and talked and talked for about 2 hours. We made so much noise that we woke up my wife and she came down to join us.

You just have to be flexible so that when they want to talk to you, you are willing to do so.

I always just put aside what I'm doing and talk to them.

John Howard – Prime Minister of Australia, Canberra

It is hard to listen to kids without preaching to them. I struggle with that myself. Do you? I love my kids and I want to fix their problems, and the more I worry about the subject matter of the discussion the worse my tendency to interrupt.

Not listening is especially an issue for teenagers. But if we don't listen they will stop wanting to talk to us. We need to 'see with both ears'.

Body language is an important part of listening.[10] Your body language can indicate that you are not really listening (e.g. 'multitasking' by continuing to read a book or a newspaper or working on a computer or PDA). Our style of listening and talking determines whether communication can occur.

It's really important to accept your children as equals and to treat them as such.

Sometimes when I was fighting with my younger daughter, she would say "Dad, I'm listening to you but I can't hear you. When you adopt that tone of voice I can't hear what you are saying. Change your tone and I will be able to hear you".

Sir Gustav Nossal – scientist, Australian of the Year, Melbourne

Good listening requires effort

Sometimes it can get confusing to talk to a teenage girl. It can seem like she doesn't want to listen. She can push you away and say awful things. It is those times that she is sometimes looking for the opposite, for a genuine listening ear.

Fathers, listen to your daughters.

Girls send out lots of messages and often those messages aren't very clear. For example daughters might say 'Go away', but what that might mean is 'Stay here. I really need a hug.'

Rosemary Kendell – occupational therapist, Floreat

For dads, listening to their teenage daughters talk about friends can be less interesting than talking about sport, and sometimes it all bewilders us. So listen to her and ask her about her life.

It's really important to engage with girls about their relationships, even if you sometimes find it bewildering.

It's important for teenage girls to be liked by their peers and therefore its important to listen to what they are saying about who likes who, who doesn't like who etc.

Jim McCluskey – medical researcher, immunologist, Melbourne

Do you 'boomerang' or harpoon?

Another common problem that occurs when we try to communicate with anyone is the tendency we all have to bring the conversation back to ourselves rather than really listening to the other person. In our family we call it 'boomeranging' versus 'harpooning'.

I have always had an urge to boomerang the conversation back to myself when I talk to someone and I have had to learn to be intentional about avoiding it in any conversation.

Boomeranging means bringing the conversation back to yourself rather than really listening. For example, I have an acquaintance who is a schoolteacher who boomerangs all the time. But she doesn't seem to notice. So I have stopped sharing anything with her.

Once I decided to risk it and try to communicate personally with her so I said once 'I have been struggling a bit at work lately with some extra work that has been given to me'. Her reply was 'Well now you know how us teachers feel!' Boomerang! Communication was killed, stone dead.

It is helpful to have a word like 'boomeranging' to describe it, because we can now, in our family, say 'hey, you are boomeranging', and we all know exactly what we mean.

An example of boomeranging is when your teenage daughter tells you about her experience travelling, you then tell her about yours. When she tells you about something that happened at school you then tell her one of your stories. This is 'boomeranging' the conversation back to yourself. It is common.

In its worst form boomeranging runs like this. 'Dad, I feel really sad about what Grandad said to me.' Dad replies: 'Well now you now how I have felt having to listen to him for all those years that I was growing up'.

Harpooning on the other hand means staying with her as she expresses her feelings, so that you continue to find out what things are like from her viewpoint, like a harpoon stuck in a whale, rather than boomeranging the discussion back to yourself (e.g. 'what was it about what Grandad did…. how did it make you feel?')

I have recently taught my own daughter this strategy as a social skill at parties after she told me that sometimes she didn't know how to converse with new friends without just blabbing on about herself all the time. I explained to her that most people that you meet will talk about themselves and not really be good listeners, so if she can develop that skill of harpooning she will be ahead of most other people and will have friends who like being with her.

Of course harpooning is listening, not 'conducting an inquisition'.

Here are some examples of boomeranging and harpooning that occur in everyday discussions:

Travel
Harpoon: Great. What did you enjoy most about the place?
Boomerang: I went there too. Let me tell you about....

Children
Harpoon: What do you find best about that school?
Boomerang: Our kids are at another school. It....

Work
Harpoon: What do you enjoy most in your work?
Boomerang: I tried that, but now I work ....

Stress
Harpoon: That's tough. How are you coping with it?
Boomerang: I feel like that too. I hate it when .....

Illness
Harpoon: I'm really sorry to hear that. Does it frighten you?
Boomerang: I had that too. None of the doctors could ...

Fathers and father-figures can learn to 'harpoon listen'. When they do, kids feel free to talk to them about anything because they know they will be heard and that it is safe to tell them anything.

Listening gives our daughters a sense of being worthwhile and valued.

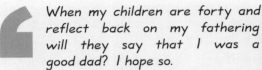

When my children are forty and reflect back on my fathering will they say that I was a good dad? I hope so.

At least I hope they will say that I was their friend and they could talk to me about anything without fear of being embarrassed or scared. Kids need that from their dads.

Ian Campbell – yachtsman,
Australian Federal Senator, Cabinet Minister, Subiaco

When we genuinely listen to our daughter we are gradually invited to enter the private spaces of her life. If she trusts us we need to be really careful with what information she gives us and how we react to her.

Don't be too critical or judgemental

Judgementalism kills communication.

> *I ask kids to rate the level of honesty with which they speak to their parents on a scale of 0-10.*
> *What we find is that the more judgmental and critical the parents are, the less honest the children are - they fear being criticised and rejected. So we ask parents to spend a whole month of playing the role of 'priest confessor', i.e. of listening without being critical (critical in words or critical in body language). That way they just listen for the whole month. There is a remarkable change, as kids honesty rating goes up to 10.*
> *But these strategies don't come naturally.*

George O'Neill – drug rehabilitation doctor, researcher, obstetrician, Subiaco

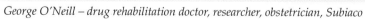

Listening as a family

Talking about feelings can also occur as a family. It is hard for kids to deal with the fears evoked by TV news. Many kids suffered exaggerated anxiety by watching the World Trade Center attacks over and over.[11] Although a family can control such exposure to some extent, children will still get exposed to fear-provoking information elsewhere. So creating an environment to discuss such fears is important in a family, especially around the meal table, watching TV or when putting kids to bed.

It is also something that father-figures, particularly in the extended family, could consider.

Here is a summary of some relevant information regarding listening as a family:

- children have many fears that are often hidden – be willing to talk about them
- families who can handle grief well together develop an extra bond because of the feeling of shared suffering
- the major stressors for children are moving house, going to a new school, divorce of their parents and bereavement, so be aware of that and talk about them
- terrorism and other things they hear on the news should be discussed openly with children
- be willing to openly discuss 'local' tragedies (e.g. death of a child at school or a grandparent)

Listening to a daughter's emotions

The fact that girls are emotional and often 'wear their hearts on their sleeve' can confuse or even annoy some fathers. It can cause them to tune out in one way or another. In the end those dads provide very little emotional sustenance for their daughters. And some dads express their frustration using words from the 'just-snap-out-of-it' school of psychology such as 'don't be silly'.

But being willing to listen to a girl's emotions reduces her risk of psychological distress.[12-14]

Here are some tips to help you make it easier to listen to your daughter's emotions:

- don't overreact to what your daughter expresses or you will probably make it worse
- when she has a broken heart, don't trivialise it
- don't assume that girls will always express their fears
- ask her to describe her feelings in words
- ask her if she is frightened of something about the situation

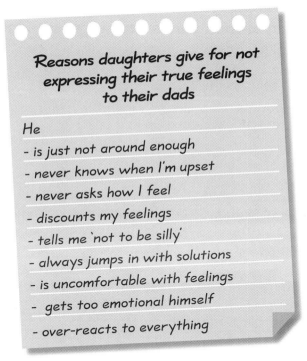

Reasons daughters give for not expressing their true feelings to their dads

He

- is just not around enough
- never knows when I'm upset
- never asks how I feel
- discounts my feelings
- tells me 'not to be silly'
- always jumps in with solutions
- is uncomfortable with feelings
- gets too emotional himself
- over-reacts to everything

Empathy

It is impossible to talk about listening to feelings without talking about empathy. Do you know what empathy is? I didn't know, for many years. Empathy[15] is about understanding what it might be like from her shoes, though you will never completely understand and you ought not actually say that you do.

Mothers typically score better when it comes to showing empathy with children.[16] When dads do show empathy it makes a difference. For example it produces greater trust[17] and the kids are less likely to have angry outbursts.[18]

Because fathers and father-figures are often fact-oriented, rational problem-solvers, this can get in the way of proper listening.

The following explanation and diagram have been helpful to many others when they were learning how to be empathic.

Listening to facts versus listening to feelings

Being a good listener is acknowledged to be a difficult skill[19] but it can be learnt.[20,21] One way to learn to improve is to learn to 'listen to the heart'.

Most communication occurs around the area of facts, such as a doctor who is required to find out facts from the patient (e.g. 'I have a lump in my breast') and then to communicate facts back to the patient (e.g. 'You need a biopsy'.)

Most communication between fathers and daughters is about facts too - 'What did you do at school today?', 'Don't forget your homework', 'When will you be home?' That is what we call 'head to head' communication.

Imagine you wake up in the morning and your daughter declares that she is not going to school that day, even though it is an important time of the school year, with exams approaching. The conversation might flow head-to-head (i.e. facts-to-facts) like this:

It is natural that most communication is like this, but the problem arises when it all occurs like that. When I communicate head-to-head, my daughter doesn't feel that she has been genuinely listened to.

> Listen to her heart, not just her words
> - such empathy means a daughter feels truly listened to

We have heads for facts but we also have hearts that feel - empathy is also about communicating effectively 'heart-to-heart'. Just as doctors should elicit from their patients relevant feelings (e.g. 'my mum died of breast cancer when I was just 16 and I am frightened') and then communicate back to the patients the fact that they care about their feelings (e.g. 'that must have been a tough time for you'), so a father can learn to communicate heart-to-heart with his daughter.

So when your daughter is refusing to go to school, instead of accusing her of laziness because there is no apparent reason, you might consider something like the following:

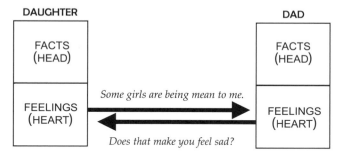

So why not think of how this might apply to you when you talk with your daughter. You might spend time discussing the facts, but then try to communicate 'heart-to-heart'. Gently find out how she is really feeling about things. And instead of evaluating those feelings ('don't be silly' etc), try understanding her feelings then showing how you feel about her situation in return.

In general, empathy could be as simple as paying attention to your daughter and being interested in how she is feeling.

It might also include appropriate touching like a hug or a gentle hand on the shoulder.

And it is generally unhelpful to simply try to diagnose and explain her feelings to her with 'you are only feeling like this because.....' and then to try to fix her problem – 'what you need to do is..........'

Here are some <u>helpful things to say</u> to kids that others find useful for expressing empathy:

- 'sounds like that is really hard for you'
- 'are you feeling anxious about what your friends are doing?'
- 'sounds like you are feeling sad about this'
- 'sounds like you are feeling left out – am I right on that?'
- 'if you could be any animal right now, what animal would you be?
- 'would a hug help?'

Some other <u>ways</u> to show empathy are:

- simple phrases ('wow, you've really been through a lot')
- legitimisation ('now I understand why you would have found that difficult')
- a rephrasing or summary of her situation ('I just want to check I have understood you correctly')
- self-disclosure ('I did experience that once myself and it got me down too') but avoid 'boomeranging'
- a comment about your own feelings ('it makes me sad to hear that')

Some <u>unhelpful</u> things to avoid saying to a child (or anyone!)

- 'don't be silly'
- 'just snap out of it'
- 'how could you be so silly'
- 'don't be childish'

- 'this business is really annoying me'
- 'you never seem to learn from your mistakes'

By indicating that we grasp their story, daughters get the feeling of being understood. That feeling can create wonderful moments of connection.[23,24]

One aspect of having a dad or father-figure who is a good listener is that daughters feel 'safe' with him. Feeling 'unsafe' can be as simple as being judged, being told why you are wrong or you are stupid. So becoming a good listener will dispel that feeling and make them feel safe when they open their mouth to speak.

It's just really nice having a dad like the one I've got because some men are really mean to their kids. They swear at them and yell at them and they are a bad influence.

Dad isn't like that. Not Dad.

Olivia Lambert – student, Maylands and Sydney

Listening to teenagers

It can be especially difficult to listen to teenagers for many reasons – they are breaking away from us and they are trying new things, many of which frighten us. And we often don't even understand what they are talking about. Yet teenagers desperately want to be listened to without being preached at.

Interestingly, the times when teenagers are the most rebellious, obnoxious and even hurtful are the times when they need the most listening to and the most love.

So dads and father-figures, be prepared to spend extra time to listen, by just sitting with her without saying anything for a while.

> *I have two daughters. To hear what is on their mind I grab a pillow and sit on the end of the bed for half an hour. The first twenty five minutes I just listen to what's happening, but it is the last five minutes that you really find out what is happening in their lives and what concerns them.*

David Bowtell – scientist, Melbourne

Because listening to teenagers is one of the things dads and father-figures find hardest to do, despite it being the time when she needs it most, I have listed some things to do that help when listening to teenage daughters:

- be patient and allow time – she is probably busy
- try to understand what it is like from her shoes
- listen shoulder to shoulder (e.g. in the car, at the sink or sitting next to each other)
- listen even if it is uninteresting to you (e.g. about her friends, her music)
- if you can't find time to listen, then cut back on something
- learn and practise some of the specific helpful phrases listed above
- realise that sometimes when she is pushing you away and saying awful things she is really wanting you to stay and listen to her

And remember, you might be her dad but you are not God, all knowing and all powerful – you can't know all the answers and you won't be able to fix everything, even though your heart might ache to do so. Knowing this, and being able to say it to your children, is very relaxing for everyone.

Interestingly, becoming a better listener has benefits to a dad. One of them is that you get better connection with your daughter. You get to understand what life is like from her shoes and you find out who her friends and enemies are, what things she fears and what she loves.[25]

Maybe now that you have read this chapter on good listening you will understand why I said it is so very hard to do it well.

It is easier to show love with hugs and words than to show love by listening to her.

It is hard to be a listener, but if it were easy then society would have more people who listen. Good listeners are rare.

Listening to girls
– some extra things to think about

Adult daughters

- were you listened to as a child?
- how does that affect your view of yourself and the value of your ideas?
- is that affecting your marriage?
- are you allowing yourself to be listened to?

Husbands

- was your wife listened to as a child?
- do you block listening in ways that are similar to what she experienced as a child?
- are you aware of the emotions that induces?
- look back through the chapter and ask yourself which of the styles of listening applies to you as a partner
- try them in your next conversation

Father-figures

- be available to be a listening ear
- it is often easier for a girl, especially in adolescent years, to talk to someone who is not a parent
- this also applies to children who are close to their parents
- look back through the chapter and ask yourself which styles of listening apply to you as a father-figure
- try some of these listening skills

What the girls need from me as their dad, is not to tell them that they are pretty but that they are special.

It really makes me proud to tell them that I think they are special.

David Gower – English Test cricket captain, commentator, Winchester

Chapter 10

Helping her realise how special she is

"*A daughter needs to hear from her dad how unique and special she is*"

CHAPTER TOPICS

- Why it is important for fathers to make girls feel special
- What being a special person really means
- How to help a daughter realise her specialness
- Having a special family
- Her special future

Many dads have a special father-daughter relationship with their girls. That is terrific, but it is not the 'specialness' that I am talking about in this chapter. I am talking about making them *feel special*. By that I mean that they have special character, a special body, special gifts, a special place in life and, importantly, a special and unique future ahead of them.

Why it is important for fathers to make girls feel special

My father made me feel attractive and capable but he never made me feel more attractive or more intelligent than anyone else. He just made me feel secure in the fact that I was worthy as a woman.

I have seen women who do not get this from their fathers and they have lots of problems, including sexual problems.

Gay Crooks – paediatric cancer specialist & scientist, Los Angeles

When I am asked 'Which of the needs of children is most often neglected by dads?', this is the one I most often discuss. Most dads don't know how to make kids feel special. I have observed that a feeling of *specialness* is one of the hardest things to achieve in our kids.

Many kids just don't feel very special. They don't feel that their existence is any *different* to anyone else's and so there is isn't much meaning in *their* life. Feeling special refers to how children feel about themselves, whether they are worthy of being loved and trusted because their life is of consequence, as well as their awareness of their own special abilities and opportunities to contribute to the world.[1,2] Do you feel special?

> *Kids all want to feel special and unique, whether they are poor or wealthy.*
>
> *They want to use the special talents that they each have. And for that to work, they have to be reminded that they are special, unique and talented.*

Rosey Grier – NFL football star,
Kennedy bodyguard and actor, Los Angeles

Fathers are in a powerful position to help each child realise that they are a wonderfully complex mixture of different personalities, skills, ideas and potentialities with a unique place in the world and a special and interesting future ahead of them.

> *The first input a girl gets as a woman is from her father, whether it is about her mind, her athleticism, her beauty, or whatever.*
>
> *He is the first man in her life.*
>
> *If you don't get told you are special by your father you will struggle for years to be able to believe that.*

Linda Carlson – actor, New York and Hollywood

There are lots of aspects about current society which make it hard for kids to feel a sense of specialness. School can be a bit like a production line. And the highly competitive nature of current society risks the possibility that children will only feel special if they achieve something special (e.g. become the top student at school or win a sporting or musical award). TV is so powerful that kids run the risk of not feeling special if they don't achieve something close to stardom.

This sense of specialness that I am describing is not a sense of chest-thumping self-importance, nor a notion that I am more special than everyone else.

> You don't have to be more special or more important than anyone else to be truly special

Feeling special is not competitive – you don't have to be more special than anyone else to be special.

A daughter's uniqueness and her special journey of life need to be recognised. Adults of my parent's generation were so afraid of making kids feel self-important that they often failed to praise their children at all in order not to 'spoil them'. But in reality, if you can really help kids appreciate their uniqueness they will feel more confident and thus more able to appreciate and celebrate the specialness of others, rather than vice versa. They will be able to celebrate the successes of others and not feel threatened by them or feel the urge to put them down.

My relationship with Dad is special because Dad makes me feel special. He always has.

How did he make me feel special? I think it was the way he spoke about me and the way he spoke to me.

I always knew I was special and my sister, Heather feels the same too. She also feels really secure in Dad's love for her.

Rosemary Kendell – *occupational therapist,*
Floreat

Most men had <u>no-one</u> who made them feel special as kids

I wonder if this failure of dads to make kids feel special is because they don't know how to. And they don't know how to because no-one ever made them feel special so they don't know what it is like or how to make it happen.

During parenting seminars I usually ask the audience 'Who made you feel special as a child?' I have now asked that question of many thousands of men and women from different backgrounds in many different settings. The frightening fact is that less than 20% of any male audience can remember or identify *anyone* at all that made them feel special as a child - not their teachers, their coaches, their grandparents, their uncles, their mother or their father. How sad is that?

Interestingly, more women can identify someone from their childhood that made them feel special than men can. That might surprise any woman who is reading this book and it might help them understand more about the men in their lives – maybe no-one made that man feel special when he was a boy. That might drive his work practices, some of his insecurities and his feelings about himself as he tries to find specialness and significance somewhere in life.

> Less than 20% of any male audience can remember or identify anyone at all that made them feel special as a child

Who made you feel special as a kid? A grandparent, youth leader, teacher, pastor, or perhaps your own father? By thinking about who did or didn't make *you* feel special as a child you will get closer to understanding how much your own daughter needs you to make her feel special because it reminds you of the feelings you had, or realise you didn't have.

Now move the clock forward 20 years and imagine that it is your daughter in the seminar room and the speaker is asking the audience who made them feel special as a kid. What do you have to do now so that she will put up her hand in 20 years time and say 'Yes, my father definitely made me feel special'? Based on what I have learnt from my audiences, the odds are only 15% at present that your daughter will nominate you. Consider for a moment how you might increase those odds.

The same thing applies to father-figures – there is less than a 10% chance that you will be mentioned. What do you need to do now as a grandfather, uncle, step-father, teacher, coach, pastor or family friend that would mean she puts up her hand in 20 years time and identifies you as someone who made her feel special as a child?

Think of the word *unique*. It's a good word to help you think of what we mean when we talk about *special*. There are unique buildings such as the Eiffel Tower, the Statue of Liberty, the Pyramids and the Sydney Opera House. These structures don't have to 'defeat' each other or any other structure to be special, they just are. There are also unique paintings, photographs, songs and many other things where we celebrate their uniqueness. Each human is like that too, and children need to be aware and enthusiastic about their unique identity.

How can a father help a young girl know that she is special?

Here are some ideas to help you as a father or father-figure to let a girl know that she is special. But first we need to discuss 'expectations' and 'acceptance'.

The three paths that fathers walk and how they affect feelings of specialness

Path 1: Expectations

Don't live out of your children.

They have their own lives, which you should encourage.

I suspect the parents of conspicuously talented children risk doing this, for example actors and athletes.

Tim Willoughby – Olympian, America's Cup yachtsman, stockbroker, Perth

The expectations path involves the attitude, often subconscious, that 'my child is here to fulfil my expectations'. This particularly occurs in fathers who have low self-esteem, who need the child to succeed to fulfil the father's dreams. And by 'succeed' I mean academically, socially, athletically, in leadership or in their beliefs.

Of course parents can rationalise such expectations as being for 'their own good', 'to be able to earn a living in the future', 'to provide for their family', 'to not waste their education', 'to not let the family down', 'it is a family tradition' etc. But if we are to cut a different path from those fathers, we need to decide whether we are willing to move on from this attitude – to accept our children and their choices as they are, not as we want or imagine them to be.

Help her see that she is here to fulfil her own destiny, not your expectations for her.

> *I had too much expectation at times of what I wanted my daughter to be rather than accepting her for who she is.*
> *I needed wisdom to understand her character and personality.*

Harley Hayward – Aboriginal pastor, Balga

Make certain that she is aware that she is not there to fulfil your own dreams. There is a terribly sad example of this in the brilliant movie 'Dead Poet's Society.'[3] One of the students who is a talented actor tells his father that he wants to have an acting career. His father, a stern, distant man tells him that it is impossible and that he must do what his family expects, enter law school. The child could not face doing that and ended up committing suicide. His father didn't accept him for who he was.

Path 2: Acceptance

This path is the 'I accept you for who you are' position. It sounds OK but it is quite passive and even reluctant. That doesn't make them feel special, it just removes the weight of expectation.

It is a shrugging of parental shoulders –'OK, so be it, I can live with it, I don't like it but I will support you anyway'. The father of the boy in 'Dead Poet's Society' could have done that. Most dads I

> Help her realise that she is here to fulfil her own destiny, not your expectations for her

know are stuck on this path. I was too. It is subtle. I thought that if one of my children was different in any way that didn't please me terribly I would be doing the right thing if I showed acceptance, rather than expectation. Even if I didn't like what they chose I would grit my teeth and work hard at accepting them for who they are.

I was proud of myself for doing that, for being accepting, but I now realise that is not enough. When I did that I showed that I hadn't switched to the third path, the path of specialness, I was blindly plodding along the path of acceptance.

The path of acceptance is a lot better than that of expectations but it still lacks something.

Path 3: Specialness

Each child is a unique and special creation. Fathers need to meet them in their uniqueness and show them how their 'traits' are unique and special e.g. to praise their flamboyance or their quiet thoughtfulness.

Everybody is like that, different and useful in their own special ways and they ought not to wish they were something else but realise the value of their uniqueness.

Kids need to know that they can't be everything.

Sam Brownback – US Senator, Presidential candidate, Kansas

There is a third path which most dads don't seem to find. This is why kids don't feel very special and why most adults have never had anyone make them feel special as a child.

On this path dads actively identify and celebrate the specialness of each child. So in the 'Dead Poets Society' example above, the father would not have just begrudgingly accepted his son's desire to be an actor rather than a lawyer but would have encouraged him, talked with him about his skills, found good schools of acting, gone to plays with him and asked him his opinion about them, been first in to the shows, sat in the front row for his performances, been first to stand up and applaud on opening night, learnt about the art of acting, laughed with him, supported him when he failed, expressed pride at his son's courageous decision, shown him that he believed in him, encouraged him by specifically identifying the areas of his acting that he thought were really good, worked with him through his limitations and kept encouraging him to follow his own unique life skills and choices. What a difference that would have made.

Children get a lot of expectations laid on them in the community to fit in and not be unique. They also get them from the media, and some kids try to develop a persona that matches someone they admire. But in pursuing that image of themselves they can end up feeling like a fake because they realise they are not really like that person. We can help them love who they really are. We want to hear our daughters say 'I am proud to be me'.[4]

So when she is with you, try and provide a different environment, one in which she can be affirmed in her difference, not criticised. Drop some expectations of her, move on from mere acceptance and begin to encourage her wonderful uniqueness.

> *If the theory that says that if fathers tell their daughters they are wonderful then they will feel good about themselves is true, then my daughter will feel wonderful. Definitely. My daughter and I are very close.*

John Howard – Prime Minister of Australia, Canberra

Don't expect your daughter to be like others

Have you ever said, or heard anyone say, in exasperation with a child, 'Why can't you be more like Rebecca?' or 'Mary does it, why can't you?' It is so easy to say that when frustrated. Have you noticed

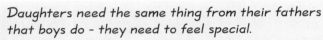

Identify things that are special about her, rather than only saying 'you're special'

that strategy never works? Kids want to feel special and unique and comparisons erode that. It infuriates kids.

> *Daughters need the same thing from their fathers that boys do - they need to feel special.*
>
> *To make a kid feel special you first have to tell them that they are special. It's very important to tell them.*

> *Secondly, you have to show them that they are unique and precious, and that there is no-one else in the world quite like them.*
>
> *Rosey Grier – NFL football star, Kennedy bodyguard and actor, Los Angeles*

Tell them they are special but identify that which is special, rather than using empty words

You need to identify that which is special in your child. Just saying 'you are so special' is better than nothing but soon it becomes repetitious and sounds hollow.

Kids, especially teenagers, can spot empty phrases and dismiss them. It is far more effective and honest to try and identify exactly what it is about your daughter that you think is special. It may be the things she does (e.g. kind things) or how she talks or laughs or her skills or creativity.

Fathers have to maintain communication with their daughters. That includes not just saying that they are special but identifying things that are special about them.

It is easy to use generic words like 'special' and 'wonderful', and doing that does mean something, but it is important to identify specific things that are special about each child such as 'I love the way you help your friends out when they are in trouble the way you do. You have a very generous way of doing that'.

Helen Reddell – asthma researcher, Sydney

Help her understand that her personality is special

There can be personality clashes between daughters and their dads, especially in teenage years. This can cause friction. Dad needs to appreciate their daughter's unique personality type, even if it annoys them. Her personality might still annoy him, and they might have a 'personality clash', but that doesn't mean he should put her down.

It is important for fathers to realise that they are not always the same and their children are not all the same, i.e. they need to understand their children's personality and deal differently with them accordingly. That will make them much more accepting because people always tend to react according to their personality type.

Graham Morris – businessman, Cairns

There are different ways of describing different personality types and although Myers-Briggs is the classic method, there are others.[5,6] Personality tests are used extensively in the corporate world when recruiting staff, although there is not a unified view of the scientific validity of each of them. The important point to make is that there are personality differences and we shouldn't try to force our daughters personality into a type that they don't already have (e.g. our own). It won't work.

Seek and value her opinion as a special, valuable contribution

Ever since I was little Dad has been telling me that I'm special and treating me with respect.

He has asked my opinion on things and asked me how I felt about things and what I thought about stuff that was going on in the house or in the world or at school.

Catherine Prout – social worker,
school chaplain, Balga

Sometimes a young woman will try to express an opinion about something to a father or father-figure but, because it is naive or ill informed, she gets put down and even humiliated. She is not asked for her opinion and is reluctant from then on to spontaneously give it, as she might be put down again.

If you do genuinely seek her opinion, she will begin to feel that her opinion is worth something – not that she is automatically correct, but that her opinion is worth listening to. She will learn how to form ideas and think through opinions.

One of the interesting things about life is that thousands of new ideas come along every day, and you should keep an open mind to allow for the possibility that your daughter will actually have some of those new ideas.

And if you encourage her to listen to the opinions of others she will be well placed to learn a lot in life. She will feel special and she will make others feel special as she listens to their opinions, too.

> My parents never gave me the impression that they were not interested in my opinions. They took everything I had to say seriously, even when they disagreed.
>
> The encouragement I received from my parents has definitely helped me be successful.

Theresa May – Chairman of the Conservative Party of Great Britain, London

This is not a trivial issue. Any failure to pay attention to her comments can have major consequences for her.

> My father has always been very authoritarian and he still is - you just can't disagree with him without upsetting him, no matter how nicely you do it.
> As kids we were never able to disagree with him and even though we are all older, with our own kids, we still can't do it - he just doesn't like it when it happens.

Grace Matthews – community worker, Sydney

My dad never asked me my opinion about anything. It wasn't a big deal for me at the time that he didn't though. There was always a gap between us.

I never had the expectation that he would show that much interest in me but I tried to attract my dad's attention all my life. I gave up because he was always busy doing other things.

Jacqui Robinson – pharmacist, Shenton Park

So invite her to comment and stimulate discussion with her (e.g. 'What do *you* think, Jane?', 'I would appreciate hearing your view of this, Rebecca.')

We were a rowdy family - we taught the kids to express their views e.g. during dinner time.

Sir Michael Parkinson – multi award-winning
British talk show host and author, Bray

Encourage her special creativity

Her creativity is special, so celebrate it. I love to see the walls of people's houses lined with pictures that the kids have painted rather than expensive showpiece pictures. They are originals but not Picassos.

I used to think that such an approach would make kids think they were more important in the world than they really are, potentially making them arrogant or at least over-confident. But in fact it is not that way at all. Displaying their creative endeavours helps them to appreciate their own specialness without them having to be the best in the world, and this seems to make them more relaxed in life.

Don't over-organise her life

To develop her special creativity, don't over-organise her life. Avoid the 'if it's Tuesday it's ballet' feeling. Over-structured lives reduce creativity. This can also inhibit development of curiosity (see Chapter 6).

> The lives of this generation of children seem very programmed, with parents taking them to sports etc.

Sharon Greenberg – occupational therapist, Seattle

Create special memories

Feeling special includes having special memories.

Work hard to create ways of remembering special events. There are plenty of tools available and creative ways of using them. These special family times provide great memories for the kids and also for their dads.

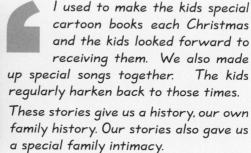

> I used to make the kids special cartoon books each Christmas and the kids looked forward to receiving them. We also made up special songs together. The kids regularly harken back to those times.
>
> These stories give us a history, our own family history. Our stories also gave us a special family intimacy.

Tom Rickman – Academy Award nominated
film screenwriter, Los Angeles

All the fathers that I spoke to who have spent time with their children making memories recall those memories with as much fondness as the children do. But it takes time.

And try to create a bit of a sense of adventure if you can – it adds to the memory.

Make a special effort on her birthday

Birthdays represent everyone's special day, a chance to be focussed on independent of everyone else in the family.

It is a great opportunity to do special things and make the day memorable or a great opportunity to spoil it by not bothering.

> On Jess's 11th birthday last week I worried as I drove home about what I could do. So I bought some nice flowers from the florist and a special birthday card. Then I wrote in the card some profound words for her. I wanted to make her feel special and that she was worth taking the time to do something special for.

Justin Langer – Australian Test cricketer, City Beach

Father-figures & specialness

Women who have identified key father-figures in their lives that made them feel special describe that feeling as very powerful. They remember affirming words and events with clarity many years later. This is discussed in more detail in Chapter 2.

For many, these father-figures are part of the family, especially grandfathers and uncles whereas for others they are schoolteachers or community workers.

> My English teacher makes me feel special. He is very supportive. He is always encouraging me to do my absolute best.
> He doesn't give any of us kids an inflated view of our abilities.
> But if I do badly in my work he goes through it all with me and helps me and encourages me.

Sarah Pocock – student, Milton Keynes

Extended family & specialness

It's hard to explain the benefits that an extended family provides children.

I believe the kids really do benefit from their relationships with the extended family.

Michael Malthouse – AFL coach, Collingwood

Fostering links with a strong, affirming extended family can make a child feel like she is part of a special tribe. It is also a way of guaranteeing that she is exposed to other father-like influences.

With such a strong background of extended family it would be hard to shake off the notion that family is important and my family is very close.

All of our children live within 5 miles of me in England, and I don't think that's a coincidence.

Sir Michael Parkinson – multi award-winning
British talk show host and author, Bray

You might consider asking those special family members to be intentional about being father-figures and you might even give them a copy of this book to help them understand how their potential role could be fulfilled.

Celebrate her uniqueness, rather than always emphasising how similar she is to others

When you talk about being a close and special family, can I remind you again to still acknowledge and celebrate the *uniqueness* of each child? Close families can fall into the trap of saying that one child is exactly like Dad and one is just like Mum. We have done that. It is far better to say that they have some characteristics that are a bit like Dad, or Mum, but that they have a whole lot more that are unique, special and different to Mum and Dad. Tell her that you are looking forward to seeing how those differences will make life evolve differently from Dad and Mum. That will be exciting and interesting, and you are looking forward to seeing it.

Create special celebrations for successes and milestones

Kids feel special if special achievements occur and are celebrated, even if they are modest. There is always stuff to celebrate in every child's life. It doesn't have to be a victory, just an improvement or a 'first'.

One of the nicest ideas I heard was that of having a family celebration for *any* success that children had. It doesn't have to be a victory, just a milestone reached. Share those celebrations equally amongst all the children. Make it a special meal at home or out, a bottle of non-alcoholic champagne and speeches. The kids love it.

If dads aren't doing it, father-figures can.

> One of the best things we have done as parents is to make a big deal about always celebrating their achievements and if there isn't a reason to have a celebration then invent one.

Ken McAullay – corporate manager, State footballer and cricketer, Perth

Be willing to create special times by doing what she wants to do

A lot of dads won't go shopping with their daughter.

I do go shopping with my fourteen year old daughter, and though I hate shopping, that's what she likes to do so I do it with her.

Jack Kingston – Congressman, Georgia

One of the things that some women described that made them feel worthwhile and special was if their father (or a key father-figure) made an effort to do things with them that they wouldn't normally be interested in. It sent a powerful and important message to them that they were worth doing that for – that they are worthwhile.

This can include activities like shopping with his daughter.

Dad has been really successful in his work and yet I never felt that we have missed out on him.

He has made us go-karts and taken us shopping.

Anna Chaney – student, Claremont

It is important to support your children in all their ventures, even if you don't necessarily enjoy them yourself at the time.

You've got to show up to 'yet another drum solo performance' even though you've heard it 100 times.

Ray Stranske – Hope Communities, Denver

Keep reminding your daughter of her own special future

Kids often feel that their own future is uncertain, worthless or scary. A father or father-figure can go a long way to encourage a sense of a special future by just saying to their child things like 'You are special and you have a very special future ahead of you – you may never become an Olympic gold medallist, a brain surgeon, a movie star or the Secretary General of the United Nations but you have a different special future'; 'I know the world will be enriched by having you around and will be better off for you having been here living on this planet'; 'There are so many people who will benefit from you and I am really looking forward to seeing how it happens'.

> Keep reminding your daughter that she has her own special future and you are looking forward to seeing it happen

I find that in my life if something I do helps just one person then it seems to make it all worthwhile. That is how I feel about writing and speaking about fathers, parenting and family life. Hearing about how some fathers' lives have been transformed by these activities makes all the hard work worthwhile.

I feel the same about my children. Their lives are intrinsically unique from the experiential point of view but they are also in a position to help other people. So I try to get them to feel that helping just one person will be enough, without having to impact on the other seven billion people on earth.

You have to ask them what they would like to do with their unique talents that would enable them to pursue their dreams, to be able to go into the 'orchard of life and pick anything'.

Rosey Grier – NFL football star,
Kennedy bodyguard and actor, Los Angeles

Help her to deal positively with the uncertainty of the future

Part of the process of encouraging her special future will be teaching her how to deal with *future uncertainty*, not just in her career but in her whole life. Help her to see life as an unfolding adventure and as a journey to be enjoyed regardless of the result at the end. Indeed almost everyone has found that the result is often a let down compared to the fun of the journey. Help her to focus on the process and not the product, the journey and not the destination.

Be careful when using threats about the future to motivate teenagers (e.g. 'if you don't study now, you will never get a job' or 'if you don't …. you won't have any friends').

Keep reminding her of her specialness and her special future, despite any ups and downs she will experience.

> The one thing I do really appreciate about my father is that he gave me the sense that I could be anything that I wanted to be, that I could do anything I wanted to do.
> We moved to North Carolina and I went to a new school where I was picked on by a girl because I was from up north and I was different.
> My dad knew that I was miserable and said something to me about this girl which I have never forgotten. He said "Ignore her. This is probably her best time in life, but your best time is yet to come. She will become faded and unhappy".
> I have since been back there and I believe he was right.

Courtenay Broaddus – pulmonologist, San Francisco

Teach her that the specialness of any job is not measurable by income

Discuss with her how, when she finds her niche, that success in that task will not be measurable by income, nor by fame, nor power nor by defeating someone else (i.e. by competition). The specialness of her work can only truly be measured by what her work means.

She can make even the most mundane work meaningful by what she chooses to do and how she does it, by how the community of workers supports each other and by the way that her community bands together to help others (e.g. raising money for worthy causes).

Give her 'special access' to you during the day

> *I had a dedicated telephone line installed that only my wife and five children have the number for.*
> *They can get me any time and thus they have direct access to me.*
>
> Frank Wolf – Congressman, Virginia

There is no doubt that kids feel special if they have special access to you. I have heard that from many children – to be able to phone dad when everyone else has to wait or be screened creates a very special feeling.

> *Once I was about to start a speech in Congress and my daughter called me on my cell phone. She told me she couldn't find her baseball glove and did I know where it was? I stopped my speech to help her find her baseball glove and then started it again.*
> *It's important for children to know they have priority access to their dad virtually any time they want it.*
>
> Jack Kingston – Congressman, Georgia

Special letters/notes to her

Whether it is a note in her lunchbox that she will read at lunchtime, a text message on her phone, an email or a specially written letter, kids really do appreciate specially written messages from fathers or father-figures. It helps to make them feel special. They often save them. It is hard to find time, focus and energy to write things down but kids really appreciate specially written, rather than spoken, words.

Messages and notes convey specialness and help fathers stay connected with their children. In that sense modern technology is the friend of good fathering, not its enemy.

When my daughter was in her final year of high school, all the parents were invited to write brief notes to their daughters to be opened and read by them at their school retreat. Almost every parent did that, but I felt very sad when I heard that some of the parents didn't write anything for their kids. Imagine how those kids felt as they sat there watching their friends reading, often in tears, those wonderful letters from their parents.

Anyway, here is what I wrote to Amy (she has given me permission to include it here). I have included the whole note because so many reviewers have enjoyed reading it and because you may be interested in writing such a note to your own daughter and want some hints. Amy said she cried when she read it the first time and I still get teary every time I read it again myself.

Amy,

You know what is coming, I think. Lots of stuff from your Dad who adores you.

I remember the moment you were born. Mum had wanted a daughter and although I was saying to myself 'another son will be OK', and he would have been, when I saw it was a girl, my heart jumped. Not just for Mum's sake, but for mine, because I already knew there was something special about dads and their daughters. And there sure is with us.

There are so many memories in the last nearly - 17 years that it almost seems silly writing them down. But I do need to list some so here goes:

- *I have already said that when you were born it was special.*

- *And all those hugs you give me: I am not joking when I come home from being away and I tell you I have ADHD- Amy Deficiency of Hugs Disorder. It really does mean a lot to me.*

- *I have loved having you sitting on my lap. You always did that as a kid, right from the beginning. You always said it was your favourite place in the whole world. And I have always said that I hope you still hug me and sit on my lap when you are older.*

- *Our trip around the world was so special. It was special for each of the boys too and our trip was differently special. Travelling together, talking, Disneyland, Universal Studios, hiring cars, being in Canada, Pittsburgh, Chicago, England and then Paris. All wonderful and I remember all of it. And I especially remember having tears in my eyes that last night in Paris when I realised it was all over, at least for that trip.*

- *I love every morning when I am downstairs before you go to school. I love just saying hello when you come home from somewhere. I will change my flights sometimes just to get home and have a half hour with my kids.*

- *I remember coming home from a long trip once in the middle of the night when you were little. When I did my usual thing of coming in to kiss my kids hello whilst they were sleeping you were actually sitting up in bed, waiting for me. You had heard the taxi arrive. How special that was.*

- *And how I loved reading you stories at night and cuddling up. Even when I come in and just sit down on your bed whilst you are reading or doing homework, and I just say nothing, I love it.*

- *Every time I take you anywhere is also a wonderful time for me (even, just maybe, taking you to rowing at 4am on cold wet mornings. Well maybe not then, but every other time).*

But those things are kind of selfish to me. It is easy to be fond of you and like you because you are pretty special: i.e. you would be that special if I wasn't on the scene.

There are lots of things that I like about you. I love your warm heart, a heart that has such love and compassion. I love your kindness towards people – it is obvious. I love the way you usually try to see the positive in things and in people rather than the negative. I love the way you are affectionate. I love your brightness and cleverness and your wise ways – you are an insightful person, beyond your years. You are attractive in every way, physically and as a person. You have a deep and wise capacity for faith. You have an amazing willingness to have a go at things – you will try anything.

This year is a big year – that's a bit of a cliché I guess. I admire how you have gone about defining your own path in life. I know that when you end up doing paid work or unpaid work you will make a big contribution to the world, I do pray that you will keep following your heart, as we have always encouraged you to do. I know you will be a community person like your mum, and that community will benefit from your compassion.

Sometime you will probably meet someone whom you wish to share the rest of your life with. I have joked that I will be like 'the father of the bride', but that is not really so. They say that a good parent "gives their children roots and gives them wings", so they can fly away having had solid nourishment as children. I hope we have done that for you. When you go, you will I hope take with you something of us, your family, and pass it on (the good stuff at least!). If you do have kids, you will be a great mum. 100% certain.

And one day you will have to finally say goodbye to me (hopefully when I am old, with a memory that is not too shot!). I hope I get a chance to say goodbye, but we are not always given that luxury. When that day comes I know you will feel sad because of the love we have shared as father and daughter, more than that, as 'Bruce and Amy'. I have tears in my eyes now when I think of that day. But that is life.

I hope after I am gone you will be energised in your future life by the love and specialness of our relationship and that although you will enjoy looking back on all the warm memories, these memories will not cause you to live in the past but will be those roots that enable you to fly with the wings we have always encouraged you to use.

I could write more. A whole book in fact. But I better stop here.

You are a very special, unique and talented girl and the world will be a better place for having you around (it already is). I love you and I will be there for you as long as I am around. I think you are wonderful.

Love, Dad

Quiz Question

Who said: "Always remember that you are absolutely unique. Just like everyone else."?

Answer: Margaret Mead – cultural anthropologist, author, USA, 1901-1978

Helping girls feel special
– some extra things to think about

Adult daughters

- think about any things your father did that made you feel special
- thank your father for any special times you shared
- look in the mirror and tell yourself what a special and unique person you are
- make a list of things that make you special, including unique experiences

---

Husbands

- what are the things that make your wife special and unique?
- tell her what special things you notice about her
- do special things with her that are unusual
- affirm the specialness of the family 'tribe' your wife comes from

---

Father-figures

- think through each thing that makes your granddaughter, niece, students etc. unique
- be intentional about asking each of them what she thinks about current affairs
- ask for her advice about things
- you are well placed to remind them that they have unique and special futures that are different to everyone else's
- tell them how much you are looking forward to seeing their future

> I enjoy doing stuff with my dad, like going on daddy-daughter dates.
>
> We go out for lunch, go see a movie, go for a jog or something - it's really nice.
>
> It makes me feel really special just to have someone I can go out with and just be myself, just chat and laugh at things.

Shiloh Blondell – student, Claremont

Chapter 11

Dad dates and special trips

"My trip away with my daughter healed our relationship - now we are close"

CHAPTER TOPICS

- Why special one-on-one times are powerful
- The value of one-on-one time
- Special trips with her
- Taking her on work trips

Why special one-on-one times are powerful

Some of the best special times are one-on-one times (i.e. no other adults and no other children). If dads make an effort to create such special times with a daughter, that can really make her feel special. It also makes her feel worthwhile because dad could spend his time with anyone, but he chooses to spend that time with her. The feeling of worth that creates is strong.

These are times that they will remember. All the children and fathers I spoke to have described how special such activities were for both of them. It is such a good idea that I have included a number of relevant quotes on the subject.

The benefits of one-on-one time include increased feelings of worth, a closer relationship, a feeling of connectedness, increased opportunities to discuss important issues such as values and better understanding of each other.

These times also create memories that last forever. I have noticed that children who give eulogies for their fathers often name special one-on-one times as their fondest memories.

This is another idea that is ideally suited for uncles and grandfathers. Since I thought about it I have started taking my niece out for dinner and this certainly creates rich times of connectedness.

The two main one-on-one ideas that I would like to talk about are :
- dad dates with your daughter
- special trips, just you and her.

Take your daughter on 'dad dates'

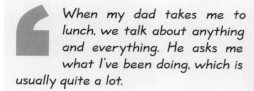
When my dad takes me to lunch, we talk about anything and everything. He asks me what I've been doing, which is usually quite a lot.

Hannah Raffel – student, Shenton Park

I cannot tell you how many daughters (and sons) have told me about how going out on dates with their fathers made them feel special, 'like a million dollars'. These dates are not meant to create another opportunity for you to have a business meeting with your daughter, to tell her things that are worrying you, to preach to her or to tell her your stories. I made that mistake initially, but my kids educated me about it. These dates are principally to listen to her, to chat or to just be together doing things.

Dad dates have a few key ingredients to succeed:

- *Only one child at a time* (if you have 3 children, go on 3 separate dates – they don't get jealous as long as they know their turn is coming later).
- *Only dad* (not mum, and not other dads with their children).
- Go to *special places* not just McDonalds each time (i.e. create special memories). I let my children choose the location of the meal for these dates, but our rule is that it has to be somewhere new. As all McDonalds are the same, we can only go to those yellow arches once then we have to find other places.
- *Use both ears* (instead of your mouth). Listen as much as possible during those dates, especially when she is a teenager. Don't make it an interrogation. Aim to laugh at least once during each date.

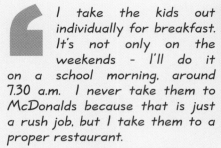

I take the kids out individually for breakfast. It's not only on the weekends - I'll do it on a school morning, around 7.30 a.m. I never take them to McDonalds because that is just a rush job, but I take them to a proper restaurant.

I know that the kids love it - it makes them feel special. Each time I take one of them the younger ones say "Take me today. I want to go too".

My 13 year old daughter is at the stage when she doesn't want to talk a lot with her dad, so I just listen. It is important to hang in there.

Neale Fong – hospital and health administrator,
AFL football team chaplain, Perth

Be intentional about dad dates and write them into your diary. These dates can help to meet many of the fundamental needs that girls have that we have already discussed - to know that you are there for them, to show unconditional love and to make them feel special.

> **Be intentional about dad dates with her and write them into your diary**

Daughters need time and attention. It doesn't have to be a long period of time but it does need to be time that is designated for her.

For example my dad has always taken me on 'dates' - we go for lunch, dinner or just out for coffee together.

It doesn't have to be a long time e.g. just an hour, but I need to know that I have his attention and that I can tell him anything that is happening in my life.

And fathers need to take an interest in whatever she is interested in. For example when they go out on a 'dad date', *dads need to take time to find out what their daughters are actually interested in.*

And he needs to be sensitive to his daughter's needs. A girl goes through a lot when she is growing up, and is often more emotional than boys, so her emotional needs need to be understood.

Catharine Ryun – White House Staffer,
daughter of Congressman Ryun, Washington DC

There is a double reward. These dad dates become special for children and for their dads.

That has been my experience. I have loved being able to sit with each of the children, my niece, my goddaughter and others, just chatting and often laughing together. When they were young we mostly ate out then went to a movie together, but since they got older this has become more varied. My wife has done one-on-one things with the kids every vacation also. We have both really enjoyed it.

But it won't happen unless you plan it. I always have to write these things into my diary.

My advice to fathers of daughters is to plan in advance to spend time with them, don't just rely on hope. Put it into your schedule. Like "on Tuesday night we will go out for dinner together".

Spontaneity and impulse are ok, but don't rely on them - don't expect to always be able to come home and say "Hey. Let's go out for dinner tonight", because it is not always convenient to do it then.

Danae Dobson – author, daughter of James Dobson, Pasadena

Take your daughter on one-on-one <u>trips</u>

> As an athlete I would take the children to other cities when I was racing. I always tried to do that one-on-one. They enjoyed travelling together, eating meals and staying in a hotel no matter what city we were in.
>
> *Jim Ryun, Congressman, 800m, 1500m and mile world record holder, Kansas*

> Dad used to take us on trips, and we rotated it between all the kids. I did a number of trips with Dad, but I remember especially going to New York City. I was about eight years old.
> Dad had to do an interview on 'Good Morning America'. We stayed in a nice hotel, went to restaurants and had breakfast together.
>
> *Catharine Ryun – White House staffer, daughter of Congressman Ryun, Washington DC*

Recently a father described to me how he had read the chapter in *Fathering from the Fast Lane* on taking kids on work trips and he had done that. It had transformed his relationship with his teenager. His teenager loved it. He also said that that trip was the best week of his whole life.

Dads, a one-on-one trip with a child is a genuine winner. I have done this with all of my three children (travelling with each of them for a whole month when they were ten years old). They represent three of the happiest months of my life. And I know it has impacted on each of the children also. When children talk about these trips they use phrases like 'it made me feel special, that I was worth something', and 'this was special because it was just Dad and me' and 'I didn't realise how nice it would be to just be with Dad for that time'.

When I think about my childhood memories and my fondest moments, my dad is in all of them.

Rachel Prout – student, Broome

It might be a work trip that you bring your daughter along to or it might be a vacation, but engineer something.

 My husband Geoff has just taken our oldest daughter on a trip around southern Spain for 5 days. She kept checking with me before they left to make sure that he had made the bookings and that he would actually go.

They had a great time together.

I think that trip was so special that it is a jewel in her life and in Geoff's too.

Fiona Stanley – scientist, Director of the Telethon Institute for Child Health, Australian of the Year, Nedlands

Traveling with the girls, even on day trips can be great. It is really nice when we take the girls up to a special event up in London, say a theatre trip, and you can just see the look of pleasure on their faces.

David Gower – English Test cricket captain, commentator, Winchester

There is something nice about skiing together and of course you get to sit on a chairlift for 15 minutes with each child talking and enjoying things together.

Those rides on the chair lift together are an important part of that.

Philip Greenberg – scientist, Seattle

It is not possible for many dads to afford things like ski trips but it doesn't have to be an expensive trip – anywhere different will do, as long as you make the effort and make it an adventure.

> *Dad was always doing things to create a strong family bond.*
>
> *We went out camping (sleeping under the stars), collected Christmas trees from the bush (they were free that way) and sat around campfires together singing/learning songs from him (and making up new verses).*
>
> *These were loving, bonding times which created a warm togetherness and an atmosphere of fun and relaxation.*

Sandy Robinson – teacher, Bassendean

Do what she wants to do, not what you want to do or what you imagine she might like.

> *I made sure that what I did with the children was what they fancied, not what I thought they needed.*
>
> *We went camping in Dartmoor and sailing on the Solent. I did that with the boys.*

> *My daughter Suzannah however preferred a trip to London shopping, going to the theatre and having a posh meal.*
>
> *Doing these things with just one child at a time has been important, partly because with only one child with me there was no sibling rivalry to deal with.*

Keith Whale – pharmaceutical company executive, Winchester and Auckland

If you travel with your work, take your daughter with you sometimes. Again, just one child at a time without any other adults.

You not only make the child feel special but you learn about her and begin to see her as a companion rather than as a daughter.

> I thought "Cool. I get to go around the world". But on reflection. I can see that Dad was really making an effort to get to know each of us as people and to spend time with us. I'm not sure that all of my friends were getting that from their dads.
>
> I am a very independent person and being so close to Dad for so long meant that he learnt to appreciate my capacity for independent thought and decision making.

Amy Robinson – student, Perth

Involving her in work trips

> I am here on this lecture tour with my twenty year old daughter Catherine. I have taken all of the kids on trips at some stage. Although we are all very close as a family and have a lot a fun together. I don't really get a lot of individual time with any one of the children when I am at home.
>
> Our family times together often sound like four radio stations all turned on at once, or four separate TV sets on playing at once.
>
> These one-on-one travel opportunities with each of my children are really the only times that I find out what is happening in their lives.
>
> I would recommend to any young father that they spend time individually with each of the children.

Bill Bryson – award winning author, Norfolk

For those dads who have to travel for their work, consider taking your kids along, one at a time. That has worked well for me and others. It doesn't matter whether it is overseas work or driving a truck around.

Here are some ideas that others have found helpful for taking their kids on work trips:

- accept that you can take your child on work trips
- she can come to your work sessions, perhaps with a game or something else to keep her entertained
- you can utilise childcare services at crucial times
- she can be looked after by partners of colleagues
- she can watch TV in the hotel room or play on a computer whilst you are working
- if you stay with friends or family she can be looked after or even attend school with their kids
- if it is a work trip, allow time to do some non-work fun things together
- be adventurous – do something extra that neither of you has done before (e.g. hire a cabin, rent a sports car, go rafting or kayaking)
- don't let her school dictate to you whether or not she is permitted to go (she is your child, not theirs, and she will benefit way more by having that trip with you)

When to take trips with kids

I don't think there is any particular age for these trips. I have done them when they were nine or ten years old. Complicated trips (e.g. overseas) require that they are old enough to take some responsibility and old enough to remember the experience. By doing it at a particular age it is easier to talk to the other kids about the fact that they are not going – they will get to go when they reach that age.

Simple trips can be done at almost any age.

Don't wait too long to do this. The kids may not want to go if they are late teenagers. And some dads regret not having done more one-on-one things with their kids.

> *Going dinghy sailing on our summer holidays or going out for a meal with my daughter at a local Chinese restaurant when she became a teenager has provided enormous fun together.*
>
> *I remember times like those as particularly special and I wish I had planned more of them.*
>
> *We've always been very strong on doing things together as a family and I think given my time again I'd like to have spent more one-to-one time with each of our children.*

Nicky Lee – author and co-founder, The Marriage Course, London

> *If I had my time all over again, I would take them away with me one-on-one on trips so that I could have time to focus on them.*

Michael Chaney – company director, Wesfarmers, BHP, Woodside, NAB, Perth

> *I didn't spend much one-on-one time with my children. In those days my then wife and I had the view that we needed to do everything together equally.*
>
>
>
> *I think it was really a bum idea. It was a stupid thing to do because it denied the individuality of individual children.*
>
> *My kids were very different and I should have done more things with them as individuals.*

Frank Pierson – Oscar winning screenwriter-director, Los Angeles

Put these dates into your diary or they might get swamped by day-to-day pressures and never happen.

'Rites-of-passage' trips

Western cultures have three main rites-of-passage ceremonies – birth, marriage and death. The one that has disappeared from most western cultures is the celebration of the passage from childhood to adulthood. Some families make up their own, often involving a special trip. I have taken each of my kids backpacking one-on-one between their primary / junior school and high school. We sit around the campfire cooking and chatting. We finish by climbing the Gloucester Tree, a 160 foot giant lookout with a scary metal ladder. These are rich times of togetherness.

<u>Father-figures</u> and these special trips

As with dad dates, some father-figures are well placed to take girls on trips. One-on-one trips are only likely to be appropriate for some grandfathers and stepfathers, but taking a girl along with your own daughter might provide special moments for you as a father-figure to talk with her.

For example if that other girl is struggling in life, being away somewhere might create opportunities to talk with her with words of encouragement that you might not otherwise get. Affirming words at special times are long-remembered by children. Such a conversation might flow like this: 'Sarah, I know you have been feeling a bit down lately about school and other things but I have watched the way you…….and I couldn't help but notice how good you are at that sort of thing. I think you have a real gift…. Using that gift in the future is going to be a real winner for you…..I really believe in you…you have what it takes to…..'

It is profoundly important to make kids feel special. I encourage you to think about creating special times with your daughter to achieve that.

> I have found that having children from two separate marriages can be very difficult.
>
> It can be emotionally rending and you can understand why men want to give up.
>
> It's very emotionally difficult.
>
> But you've just got to fight this and get involved.

Peter Hillary – mountaineer,
son of Everest pioneer Sir Edmund Hillary, Auckland

Chapter 12

Difficulties and blocks

"Dads remain important after separation, even though it becomes more difficult"

CHAPTER TOPICS

- Why it is important to consider blocks that fathers have

- Handling separation

- What if your dad wasn't a good role model?

- Other reasons why being a good dad is hard for some men

- Apologising to your daughter

Why it is important to consider blocks that fathers have

A lot of men have roadblocks to being good dads. These blocks may be generated by a father's own role model of fathering, by his life circumstances or by illness, busyness, mental health issues and many others. I suspect we all have some of these roadblocks to some extent.

Unless we acknowledge them, how can we deal with them?

We might end up failing as a dad because we haven't overcome these blocks. For example we might say things like 'I can never be a good dad now that we are separated', or 'with a father like mine I can't possibly be a good dad' or 'what my kids really need is food on the table and school fees, that's why I don't have time for them' or 'you can't learn about fathering from books and courses – that stuff is all rubbish. You can only learn on the job, from your mistakes'.

Daughters might consider how these issues might have influenced their father's parenting and might even show him this chapter and invite him to talk about.

I know I can only provide a glimpse of some of these roadblocks here.

Handling separation and divorce wisely

There is plenty of published data supporting the notion that dads remain important after separation, even though it becomes more difficult.[1,2] All kids, girls as well as boys, do statistically better socially, at school, in their mood and in their behaviour if dads stay involved after separation.[3-8]

Separation from the children and from the family unit doesn't need to be an insurmountable problem. Many separated dads have described to me how they became even closer to a daughter after separation because of lifestyle, work and personal changes that they had made.

> I worked long hours and never really saw my daughters. Then we divorced and I had to spend time with them. I realised then how much fun it was. I loved it.
>
> I just wish I had realised that earlier.

John Treebrook – stockbroker, Wembley

In fact this is one reason why the published statistics lack accuracy – the term 'fatherlessness' is too vague because many separated dads are very connected with their children and many at-home fathers are not.

But staying connected requires sacrifice and a willingness to work hard to overcome the difficulties that separation brings to fathers.

> If you're a separated father, there's a fair bit of selflessness involved.
>
> Eventually, when you get the into the habit of saying 'I've got the kids', you start going back to what you wanted to do initially with your own life anyway. After all, we've all got our hopes and ambitions, and stuff like that. But you've now taken the kids on board.
>
> Somewhere along the line you've got to get the fathering straight and then later on get out of life what you want.

Andy Byrne – grano worker, floor sander, Myaree

Almost everything suggested in this book is applicable to dads whether they live in the same house as their daughters or not. Although it can be difficult at times, the needs that daughters have for their dads doesn't change. Indeed in many cases divorce increases this need.

How you handle your divorce can have a profound effect on your kids. Dads can help build a bridge over the family rift, a rift that can otherwise be seen as abandonment.[9,10]

Here is a list of tips that separated dads have found helpful when thinking about what to do in your relationship with kids after separation (and for which there is general support in the published literature).[11-14]

> How you handle your divorce can have a profound effect on your kids

Tips for dads on *how you relate to kids* after separation:

- don't give up trying to be a good dad even though it might be hard to say goodbye to them
- let them know you will be OK
- follow the tips in this book - everything listed here is equally relevant to separated dads (though some tips, like how to spend time with kids, will obviously depend on your shared parenting arrangements)
- let your children know that you will always be there for them, for the long haul, no matter what
- show respect for their mother, even if you don't get on with her at all
- discuss personal issues with their mother in private
- don't criticise their mother in front of them
- avoid the 'good cop, bad cop' trap – don't avoid disciplining them; be a parent rather than a pal

Make sure your daughter knows you still love her despite the separation

We all need to know that there is someone who will be there for us if we need them, someone on our side in life. You can see how hard it is for kids whose dads drift out of their lives after separation.

Your daughter needs to know that your love will never cease, that you are on her side no matter where you live and whom else you might marry.

About a quarter of children whose parents are separated have little or zero contact with their non-resident parent, usually their father, and less than 10% are in shared parenting arrangements.[15] One study showed that 40% of separated dads had not seen their kids in the year prior to the study.[16] Fathers have little contact with their children if there is major parental conflict or if they live far apart. Where the father does have little contact with the child, it is not always the case that the mothers feel relieved - nearly half of resident mothers think that there is not enough contact between the child and their father.[17]

It's hard to ask me whether my children need a father-figure in their life tonight because I am really frustrated at the moment.

I ask my husband to spend some time with the children but he doesn't seem to realise how important it is. It really frustrates me.

My kids ask me "Why isn't Dad around. Does he hate us kids?"

Zenzil Read – sole parent, Denver

I stood watching a wedding in a beautiful garden setting. The bride's father, a pastor, had run off with another woman from his church when she was just a toddler. He had virtually never seen her since then, nor even maintained contact.

He would do heartless things like call her when he was going to be in town for a few days and promise that he would contact her, then never call. She would wait, listening to the phone, but he just wouldn't get around to it.

She had idealised him in her mind, somehow blaming her mother for forcing him to leave and her stepfather for not being her father.

If a man leaves the family home and a daughter, he must work hard at staying connected. The price of not doing so is too high for a young woman to pay.

Harold Bone – architect, Amsterdam

Staying in touch despite separation

Please continue to stay in touch with your child after separation, no matter how hard that is.

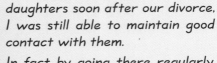

> *I can't understand how some fathers don't see their children after they are divorced.*
>
> *Although my first wife moved to Hawaii with my 2 daughters soon after our divorce, I was still able to maintain good contact with them.*
>
> *In fact by going there regularly, having them come to visit me here and always maintaining close contact with them, we have all remained very close.*
>
> *You've always got to be there for your daughters. I am very close to them and I am always there for them. They know that.*

Pat Bowlen – owner of the Denver Broncos, Denver

Here are some specific tips on staying in touch with children following separation:

- stay in contact with your kids when you are away
- always keep your promises to the kids
- be punctual for scheduled times with them
- use email and texting to stay in touch
- build up new traditions with your kids, e.g. growing a garden together, watching waves crash during storms and toasting marshmallows on open fires
- make a special effort to be there during their tough and emotionally difficult times
- teenagers especially need to see that you are there for them, despite the separation
- as the kids get older, be willing to work around their busyness to spend time with them

- don't use your kids as your major source of entertainment – develop new friends & interests
- establish equilibrium in your own life - move on and establish a new life, with new friends and activities

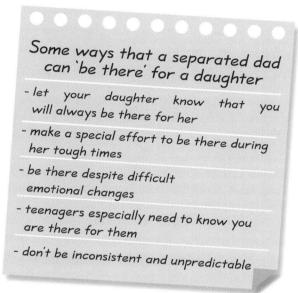

Some ways that a separated dad can 'be there' for a daughter

- let your daughter know that you will always be there for her
- make a special effort to be there during her tough times
- be there despite difficult emotional changes
- teenagers especially need to know you are there for them
- don't be inconsistent and unpredictable

Finally, stay involved with the 'mundane' things in her life. Ask about how her schoolwork is going, her friends and her celebrations. Don't just attend the 'big events'.

The richness and joy that separated dads can feel doing simple things with kids is highlighted by a conversation that took place in my hospital not long ago. On a busy night in the Emergency Department a young doctor was talking to one separated father of an 8 year old girl. He had just found out that she had been killed in a traffic accident.

The dad had stayed involved in the girl's life after his separation, including in the little things of life. So he did not sit there raging against the driver, nor talking about his girl being 'dead', or that she had stopped breathing. Instead he talked of 'his little girl', the child who had run home from school delighted with her certificate for winning a swimming race. He talked of watching her grow up, even though he would never be able to do that again. He talked of the joy and pride she had brought him in his life.

He cried as he spoke and so did the young doctor.

I am sure there is no amount of money that father would exchange for those times with his daughter. You never know how long you have a child for, so don't postpone these things.

Overcoming the role modelling of a difficult father

Men who have had a poor role model for a father can find it really hard to know what to do as a dad and to avoid repeating the same parenting behaviours themselves.[46]

You may already be trying to do your fathering differently from your own father or at least trying to get some ideas on how you can best meet the needs of your daughter in the absence of such information.

It does require a lot of thought to understand how your own fathering is affected by your experience of your dad. Such insight rarely comes quickly but is built up with each fathering 'event', especially emotional ones. Then you understand how you are programmed by your earlier experiences.

It can be very subtle. If you don't try to understand these things you might struggle to change. But you can choose to parent differently from your own dad.

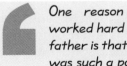

One reason that I have worked hard at being a good father is that my own father was such a poor role model. He made me feel that I was never good enough and I was always afraid of him. I ran away from home at 15 years of age to get away from him. Because of that experience I have reacted against it and have tried to be the good dad that my father never was to me.

Peter Prout — farmer, soldier, lecturer in Education, teacher, pastor, Subiaco

No dad has a harder story than Tony Cooke. His dad was abusive and a serial killer who terrorised our city for a while when I was young. His father was eventually caught, confessed and was executed for indiscriminately killing at least eight people.[18]

Those murders frightened every family in the city for months so you can imagine the sort of hard time Tony had in the school playground.

He also had no other consistent and powerful father-figures to fill that gap in his life left by his father.

He believes very strongly, and lives out those beliefs, that you can choose what sort of dad you will be regardless of your background. He is a clear example of how you can choose to break the cycle of poor fathering.

My advice to young fathers is the following: As a father, don't expect to be the same as your father. In fact that's an active choice you have to make - choose not to expect to be like your father. If your father was a fantastic father you don't have to expect to be as good as him.
If your father was terrible you don't have to assume that you are going to be terrible.
Men can choose to be different to their own dads and they should.

Tony Cooke – social worker, President of the W.A. Trades and Labour Council, son of serial killer Eric Cooke, Perth

I decided not to make the same mistakes as my parents. You've got to break the sequence.
Is Bill Clinton going to screw up his parenting of Chelsea because his mother lived in a trailer park drinking six-packs? It is hard to know.
But you can break the cycle.

Richard Feldman – music producer, Los Angeles

The first thing is to recognise the effects of your father's poor role modelling on you. You can get surprised when you become a dad how much you

> **Men can choose to be different from their own dads**

really do parent like your own dad, even though you may not want to. It helps to be open to seeing when you are acting like him. Sometimes it might be your partner who sees it rather than you, which requires from you that same openness and willingness to listen and see that you are doing the same things your own father did.

Some dads had no father at all, nor any father-figures to replace a missing father. This can make it harder also.

> *I couldn't learn fathering from my father because he took off when I was 3 months old. My mother never remarried. She struggled a bit with it but she had a good job which reduced the economic worries.*
> *I didn't have any other father-figures, no teachers or anyone like that.*

Sir Chris Bonington – mountaineer, Cumbria

Don't be afraid to acknowledge and reveal your struggles and failures

> *If I had my time over again I'd like to have shown my flaws more and not always tried to be seen to be infallible. I need to have taught them that it's OK to be fallible.*

Tim Willoughby – Olympian, America's Cup yachtsman, stockbroker, Perth

When I talk to dads about how they are going with their fathering, some seem to instantly go into defensive mode and can't ever acknowledge any problems, struggles or failures in their lives. It is as though their life is a house of cards and to admit to struggling might bring it all tumbling down.

It is OK for dads to show their failures to other dads and to their kids and to not try to look perfect or be a hero.

If dad can admit that he struggles then he can begin to learn from his friends how to improve.

Kids also benefit if dad is willing to become a bit more open. It is a great idea to tell all your failure stories to the children. My kids love telling others about their dad's many mistakes, ranging from when I nearly burnt down my parent's house when I was 10 years old to when I push-started my car one morning only to see it move forward, without me, and crash through the neighbour's fence, coming to a halt in the middle of his yard. They laugh and laugh.

Not only do a dad's mistakes encourage children, but the children get to know their dads better. To be 'known' by your children as a person, not just as their parent, is very bonding. How well do your children really know you?

So tell them openly about the times when you messed things up.

More importantly, letting kids see our struggles and failures in life shows them that struggles are not the end of the world. This models resilience.

> *Don't hesitate to show your kids who you really are, to share your own story with them, to let them know of your own doubts, fears and struggles and to thus let them know you as a person.*
> *Don't try to be a false hero but be honest.*

Peter Prout – farmer, soldier, lecturer in Education, teacher, pastor, Subiaco

Not only does it help kids to see your imperfections, but if you think about it, if you were a perfect parent it would be counterproductive and probably not very attractive to the kids.

> *Perfect parents would drive children crazy.*

Baroness Virginia Bottomley – British Member of Parliament, Secretary of State for Health, London

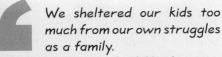

> We sheltered our kids too much from our own struggles as a family.
> We had financial difficulties at times, and also difficulties with grandparents.
> We should have discussed it with them, and let them see how we worked through it.

John Bernbaum – international consultant, Washington DC

The opportunity to show your own struggles to the kids may not actually arise easily in life - it might sound contrived. If you think this is necessary, be willing to spend time and find opportunities to tell your story.

Explaining your struggles to your kids is especially important if your failures are very public. They could be public in your local community or wider, but you shouldn't pretend that they are not there. Your kids at least need some answers to be able to give kids in the school playground and they will also benefit from a clear and honest discussion and a willingness by dad to apologise and to change his behaviour.

> I decided we had to bring Chelsea into our whole family counselling.
> Sooner or later, every child learns that her parents, or his parents, aren't perfect.
> And that's a terrifying enough thing, you know, when your kid knows you're not perfect anymore.
> This went way beyond that. And I finally decided the only way to get to where we needed to go was to level with her and let her work her way through it with us, let her draw her own conclusions and trust her. It worked pretty well.
> She's a remarkable person, my daughter.

Bill Clinton – US President, discussing the Monica Lewinsky affair[163]

Sometimes sharing your difficulties in marriage might be helpful in the family. This is a complicated area because sometimes it is appropriate and helpful and sometimes it is not. That depends upon the struggle, the way the parents deal with it and the personalities of the children. But some fathers certainly felt that describing such struggles could equip children for the future.

I would go off to nightclubs and 'played around' with other women. She found me out.

We were separated for 4 months and almost got divorced. But that point for me was like waking up from a bad dream. Things changed between us and our marriage has been brilliant ever since. We have spoken to our kids about that time.

Kids need for their parents to be honest, to explain that life is not always going to be perfect all the time.

Ray Orr – tugboat crewman, pastor, Shoreham

I think it is helpful if children can see that parents can have differences of opinion and different ways of seeing things and be comfortable with that.

That way, children can learn how to resolve problems and get some closure.

Mike Lotze – surgeon and scientist, Pittsburgh

This might include a failure in business.

> I felt that my business failure meant that I wasn't the hero to my kids that I was before.
> It, and other personal issues, caused a strain in our marriage and we separated for about 9 months. The moment that we decided on separation was one of the most horrendous times of my life, especially when it came to discussing which child would go with which parent.
> Joan and I had some wonderful counselling and we have been back together now for many years and our relationship, if anything, is stronger than it has ever been before.
> We hope that our experience of working through the difficulties is a good role model for the kids.

Ian Brayshaw – champion sportsman, TV journalist, author, Melbourne

Don't be reluctant to learn about fathering

There is a bit of a tendency amongst some men to think that good parenting just happens without the need to read or be taught anything about it. After all, there have been no fathering books available for most of human history in tribes and villages and we seem to have done OK as a species to this point.

I used to feel that way and still tend to react that way often. That sort of feeling seems to be innate in me and in many of my friends.

> I was highly resistant and refused to read any books or go to any courses. I don't really know the reason for this resistance. I guess I'd worked so hard during the day that I didn't want to come home and think about fathering as work.
> That was a mistake. If I had my time all over again I'd do it differently.

Allan Chapple – Principal of Trinity Theological College, Leederville

The feeling that fathering is all 'natural' is especially present amongst dads whose own dad did a good job - it feels intuitive for them. But many other men who had poor role models for fathers have told me they are desperate for help (e.g. from books, seminars and courses).

The tendency for men to be reluctant to read any books about fathering is also not surprising considering how many men don't like to read any assembly instructions or ask any advice (e.g. when they are lost). But the price for mis-assembling a toy bike is trivial compared to the price of finding out too late that you failed to provide what your daughter really needed from you.

Society has changed and we, as dads, must change with it or we run the risk that our children will miss out. The main changes that challenge us as dads now are:

• *The risks that kids face today are greater*

Kids of today face risks that our father's generation never really thought of, such as drug addiction and exposure to internet pornography.[19] Drugs are freely available to all teenagers today.[20] If you, as a father, don't get informed, you increase your daughter's vulnerability.

• *There are now fewer 'rules' and moral inputs from community groups*

Societies until recently have had rigid religio-cultural rules of behaviour that were heavily imprinted in children (e.g. rules about honesty, respect for elders, respect for authority, sexual behaviour and community responsibility). These rules were delivered by social groups such as Girl Guides or religious groups such as churches, synagogues and youth groups. But such influences have diminished in our society. For example church attendance has fallen from around 75% to 25% in many communities in the past 50 years.[21] Attendance at Scouts and other organised children's groups has similarly fallen.[22]

It is hard for parents to get kids to attend many of these sorts of groups now, no matter how hard they try. Thus children are now not as readily exposed to codes of behaviour or the rituals associated with those codes. So if parents are not active in their children's lives it can lead to a 'values vacuum'.

• *The media is a far more powerful influence over children today*

The power of the media over girls is well described[23-27] and I worry about the messages my own kids get from the media, plus the internet and movies.

A recent study of 1293 high school students showed that the majority spend around 18 hours per week watching television and 30 hours per week on computers (internet, chatting, homework and games).[28] They will therefore inevitably absorb the values sold on TV and the internet. If we are not active in our children's lives those values will be unopposed and these other influences will then become dominant.

• *How we live has changed – we are parenting in isolation*

We used to live in tribes and villages where parents didn't have to take all of the responsibility for childrearing – the whole village helped (uncles, aunts and grandparents were around all the time).[29] But now we live in nuclear families, or separated families, away from our own parents and siblings. Our kids have little exposure to their grandparents. So dads, we simply have to do our share of the parenting or that important fatherly influence will be missing.

Learn to be a better dad

Fathers, if we accept that we can improve as dads, we need to get on with it. We ought not be distracted from improving our fathering by anything. We especially need to avoid the notion that work is more important than our children. One of our main purposes in life as fathers is parenting our children well – for most of us they will outlast the results of our work.

> Children are our legacy. They are what you leave behind in this world.
>
> Unless you are Beethoven, Einstein or Picasso, no-one is really going to remember you after a few years.
>
> It is only the family you leave behind that are your true legacy to the world.

Sir Rod Eddington – Chief Executive, British Airways, London

Don't lie to yourself as a way of dealing with your busyness and your failure to be the father that you could be. I tend to over-rationalise my own busyness and I hear similar things from other busy men.

Thousands of men have reported being surprised at how much they have learnt about being a better dad from courses, books and seminars on fathering. Having attended reluctantly, they return home enthused. These books and courses have been shown to measurably improve father involvement and parenting skills.[30]

But be aware that intentions to change can fade fast. Reading a book like this might create temporary enthusiasm but it is easy to slip into old habits, and the next thing you know the kids have left and you are almost too late.

To avoid forgetting what I need to do as a dad, I find it helpful to write things into my diary, to keep a copy of a fathering book close by to re-read regularly (e.g. in the toilet) and to meet regularly with other men to discuss our fathering (I have been meeting for years with three other men over breakfast every second week).

Interestingly, *being a better dad is good for dads* as well as for kids. For example, better fathering usually improves marriages[31] and helps fathers grow personally themselves.[32]

Don't delay better fathering until the kids are older. It is well described that men learn too late that they really want a close father-daughter relationship, often just as she is leaving home.[33] I have seen that many times as a doctor.

One of my prime motivating factors in writing this sort of book is the feeling of sadness I get when I talk to men with cancer who are dying and they say 'I wish I had spent more time with my kids'. Those are poignant moments.

And dads do die unexpectedly, as happened to three of the men I interviewed several years ago for an earlier book (referred to in the dedication of this book and quoted in this book). I know all of their children and it is reassuring to know that those three dads did such a great job of parenting before they died. You can't assume you have forever.

Kids can die unexpectedly too, as has happened to two of the children of fathers I have interviewed, one of acute illness and one in an accident.

Don't postpone trying to be as good a dad as you can be - failing might add additional pain after such events.

 It never really entered my head that one of my children might ever die. It only happened to other people.

But she is dead, and she was only eleven.

I am angry at the school that let her fall off that rock.

But I am also angry at myself - all those years when I worked 12 hour days, leaving so early that she was asleep and coming home so late that she was asleep again. I just couldn't say 'no' to anyone.

I'll never live like that again.

But it's too late for me and Anna.

John Phillips – tradesman, San Francisco

Other problems that block good fathering

It is helpful to consider other sorts of problems that dads can struggle with that make it hard for them to do a good job as dads. Understanding such problems can be helpful for dads but also helpful for women to understand their own fathers. These include:

Time and travel problems
- extreme, unrelenting busyness
- being away from home a lot
- obsessive focus on work
- lack of mental energy when arriving home
- working from home without boundaries
- moving house regularly

Personal issues
- success, wealth or fame not well managed
- mental illnesses that are draining
- unresolved grief about family, work or other things
- being uncomfortable dealing with psychological issues
- being too chronically stressed to focus on a daughter
- low personal self-esteem
- cross-cultural clashes with daughters
- disability
- psychological issues such as:
    - depression (just can't see anything good or hopeful in her)
    - anxiety (leading to nagging and over-control)
    - obsessive-compulsive problems (just can't tolerate mess, disorganisation or dreaminess)

Fathering issues
- no insight into the role of fathers

- feeling like a failure as a dad and giving up
- trying to be a perfect, heroic dad and not showing vulnerability
- feeling hypocritical, thus avoiding discipline
- being impatient for results
- being too quick to solve or judge and never listening
- perfectionism that can't tolerate mistakes
- refusing to ever apologise for your imperfections
- beliefs and values that get in the way of fathering
- treating fathering like a chore

APPARENTLY, ACTIVE FATHERING IMPROVES WORK EFFICIENCY BY UP TO 25%. THEREFORE I'VE DECIDED TO GIVE IT A GO. SO... UM... YOU WANT TO PLAY?

There is not space here to discuss them all, but just being aware of them and thinking through these problems is half the battle. Ask your wife, a friend or even your daughter to read through them with you and discuss which ones might be, or might have been, causing difficulties. More information for fathers and father-figures on these problems and how to deal with them can be found on the book's website.

Sometimes things are too hard and dads give up. Others work hard at it but feel guilty because they have the insight to know what they should be doing but struggle to find time to do it.

 Even for competent men, fathering remains the scariest area.

It exposes their deepest fears of inadequacy.

I should know, because it is my area of fragility.

Tim Costello – lawyer, pastor, Mayor of St Kilda, Director of World Vision, Australia

The key thing is to acknowledge that such blocks can exist and to deal with each of them.

During the interviews I was impressed by the number of dads who had overcome these sorts of problems to become great dads.

But in the end these are only *potential* roadblocks - if they are acknowledged and dealt with they can be overcome to enable dads to have a deeper, more helpful, more rewarding relationship with their daughters.

How communities of men can change

It is not just individual men who can change, but men in communities who can improve their fathering. Community groups such as schools, churches, sporting and other groups can be agents to change the quality of fathering that children receive. This has been shown to be effective.[34]

Fathers, father-figures and mothers can all encourage their communities to promote good fathering. For example, they might organise fathering seminars, promote the role of father-figures, hold father-daughter dances or retreats, provide fathering resource material, list websites and tips in newsletters and hold fathering discussion groups.

Our Fathering Project Group has made a useful high quality video called 'What Kids Really Need from their Dads' which can be obtained via www.thefatheringproject.org for this sort of school or community seminar or for private viewing.

Discussion groups can be very effective. For example, one of the most memorable bits of feedback I received following a seminar was from a woman who told me that her husband and two friends had responded to the challenge of meeting regularly to discuss each chapter of *Fathering from the Fast Lane*.

> My husband took some of his friends from work to a Mens' Breakfast at our church a few months ago. He has been reading the book ever since and meeting with his friends to discuss it over breakfast.
>
> He has been transformed as a father.
>
> And it is the same for the two friends that he took along from his work.

Diane Mitchell – homemaker, South Perth

I nearly shed a tear when I heard that.

Men and women who are committed to good fathering can transform a community, and when they do they will see less bullying and violence, less risk of drugs and suicide and better attitudes to school, other kids and the future.

The most successful community groups are not intimidated by the fact that a significant percentage of the children in that group have no father to bring to parent events. They provide alternative strategies (e.g. kids can come with grandfather or significant father-figure). They also acknowledge that some families might have complicated step-father/father arrangements and avoid being prescriptive.[35]

Community groups (e.g. churches and schools)[36] can also have a measurably positive influence in providing information and social skills in areas of values and sexuality.

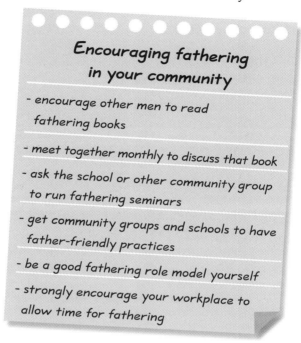

Encouraging fathering in your community

- encourage other men to read fathering books

- meet together monthly to discuss that book

- ask the school or other community group to run fathering seminars

- get community groups and schools to have father-friendly practices

- be a good fathering role model yourself

- strongly encourage your workplace to allow time for fathering

The need to better understand fathering is an issue in all countries

Initially I wondered if it was only in my own culture that fathers needed encouragement and ideas to improve their fathering, i.e. if we were a bit unusual. But the need to provide ideas and encouragement to fathers to help them improve their fathering is a world-wide issue. The published literature on the subject supports that and I have also found that in my interviews. That makes this sort of book widely necessary.

I mentioned earlier that I interviewed people from over 15 different countries in all six continents. Their issues are remarkably similar.

Therefore please think about encouraging fathers in whatever community you live in.

America is not the sole owner of bad parenting. I have seen breakdown of the families in Latin America, Australia and other places.

Dean Hirsch – International President, World Vision, Los Angeles

I think fatherhood needs a bit of a kick along in this country. It really does.

John Howard – Prime Minister of Australia, Canberra

I believe that the absentee father is one of the greatest problems we have in the culture of Western nations.

James Dobson – psychologist, author, founder of Focus on the Family, Colorado Springs

If I wanted to transform fathering in the UK I would make sure that the key leaders in our community lived out the message that fathering is important.

Jack O'sullivan – Fathers Direct U.K., London

We all have trouble spending enough time with our children during the week.

John Kolbe – physician, Auckland

China is developing very fast. Competition is strict for young fathers. In this situation, to advise the busy young fathers to look at their kids becomes extraordinarily important.

Bingci Liu – Professor of Molecular Biology, Beijing

Benefits to a dad if he makes an effort

I have not taken certain jobs and I have avoided particular trips just to be with my children.

And the 'dirty little secret' about all of this is that it is the most rewarding experience of your life - it's really good stuff and it's also fun.

Roland Warren – President of the National Fatherhood Initiative, Washington DC

There is ample evidence that a father's personal life, relationship with his wife and productivity at work can all benefit by the choices he might make to be a better father to his daughter.

Parenting is one of the most difficult and rewarding jobs we will have in our lives.

I get much more out of my relationship with my daughters than they ever get from me.

Kim Beazley – Leader of the Australian Labor Party, Canberra

Overall, the *benefits* to a dad of improved fathering include:

- greater enjoyment of life – you find 'the child within'
- better productivity at work (up to a 25% *increase*[37])
- special memories of times with the kids
- a stronger marriage – your wife is less stressed
- friendship with your kids and lots of laughter
- greater meaning in your life – work alone can seem empty and meaningless at times
- rediscovering 'how to play' and have fun
- being better connected to your community, e.g. the children's school and other parents
- feeling more relaxed and healthier – less stressed
- being less 'stale' and more creative at work
- not feeling lonely – men who overwork are lonely
- becoming a more interesting person – it can be boring just talking about work and sport

Be willing to apologise to a daughter

No father is a perfect father, so be willing to apologise to your daughter. You probably aren't perfect. Despite the best of intentions, you will make mistakes. Be willing to see

Dads, be willing to listen and apologise to your daughter, at any age

those mistakes and apologise to her at any stage of her life. Stubborn resistance and a refusal to apologise will only make things worse.

Dads, be willing to listen to your daughter when she talks about her experience of life with you. Read this book with her. And apologise to her, at any age, for anything that you might have done, probably mostly out of ignorance. Open your mind to anything you can apologise for – it is very healing for her and for you and can lead to a better relationship.

> I was too judgemental and I flirted with perfectionism. I tried to back off but it was difficult. I have since discussed this with my daughter and apologized.

Herb Stein – Emmy Award nominated director of 'Days of Our Lives',
Los Angeles

But not every father can bring himself to do that.

> My daughter wants me to apologise for ignoring her when she was young. I don't want to do that. I don't like to go back over all of that stuff.
> I did the best I could as a dad.
> My own father was never around. I never had any training or any books to learn from.
> I love her and did the best I knew how.
> I don't want to talk about all that stuff because you can't change the past anyway. What's the point of going back?

Charles Elm – pilot, Cape Town

The greater the hurt, the harder it is for fathers to apologise.

> My hope was that he would acknowledge the fact that he sexually abused his daughters and apologise to us. That he would say "Listen you are right, what I did was wrong. Please forgive me. I am ashamed of what I did". But he never ever did that.

Lucy Christmas, occupational therapist, Canada

Quiz Question

Who said: "Saying sorry is the hardest thing in the world. But you must learn to say to your children 'I am so sorry for what I said. Would you give me another chance?'"?

Answer: George Foreman – world heavyweight boxing champion, b.1949

It can be a hard road for daughters who have to deal with the consequences of your performance as a dad. That is not the case for all daughters but is certainly the case for many. The wounds caused can be deep and their effects can be profound, especially in their marriages and their mental well-being.

If you love your daughter and want the best for her, be willing to recognise and acknowledge your mistakes and apologise to her. Fathering failures can be as 'simple' as having been too busy to spend time with a daughter, or overdisciplining her, or as 'severe' as abuse. Regardless, it is really, really difficult for most men to acknowledge that they bear the responsibility for their actions or inactions. It is true that there are many factors which may have contributed (e.g. poor role modelling, extreme busyness, separation or mental health issues) and it can help your daughter if she understands what those factors were, but you have to take responsibility.

> If you love your daughter and want the best for her, be willing to recognise and acknowledge your mistakes and apologise to her

You can help your daughter move on and grow from her hurt if you 1) take responsibility for your actions and 2) apologise to her without retreating behind excuses. That allows healing for your daughter and for yourself. You and she can then live the rest of your lives in the peace of honesty, and in some cases forgiveness, rather than in the loneliness of dishonesty and stubbornness.

Forgiveness can follow if you acknowledge your responsibility and sorrow for the harm caused by your actions, behaviour or omissions.

It would be sad to die unforgiven and lonely.

I have heard many women tell me that when their fathers are lying on their deathbeds they still aren't able to admit their mistakes and apologise to their daughters.

Yet the daughters can see in their father's eyes a pleading look, wanting to say sorry to their daughter. But they just can't do it, so they die unforgiven.

Some of the daughters say "It's all right, Dad", but that is not enough. .

It's awful for a father to die unforgiven. Fathers need to learn to say sorry to their daughters. It is important for both of them.

Christabel Chamarette – clinical psychologist, Fremantle

Quiz Question

Who said: "I resolved many years ago that it was MY obligation to break the cycle – that if I could do anything in life, I would be a good father to my girls."?

Answer: Barack Obama – US Senator and Presidential candidate, b.1961

Overcoming blocks – some extra things to think about

Fathers

- don't let separation block your relationship with your daughter, whatever the circumstances
- think through how your own father is influencing how you father
- a poor fathering role model should not determine how you father – you can choose to be different
- accept that you can't be perfect so be open to learning about fathering
- be willing to apologise to your daughter
- attend and promote fathering seminars
- read and re-read fathering books

Adult daughters

- consider sympathetically whether any of these roadblocks might have applied to your own father
- talk to him about them
- encourage dads in your school and community to attend fathering seminars and read fathering books

---

Husbands

- be willing to try to understand the difficulties your father-in-law might have had as a dad rather than just getting angry with him

---

Father-figures

- consider whether any of the roadblocks listed in the chapter are stopping you being a positive father-figure
- encourage men to attend fathering seminars and read fathering books
- attend father-daughter events with her if her dad can't be there

> Adult daughters should remind themselves that they did not cause the difficulty, rejection or abuse that they may have experienced with or from their father.
>
> Neither do they need to be held captive by their hurtful experiences.
>
> They can have a role to play in their own restoration.
>
> It is possible that they can then live more freely.

Phyllis Prout – clinical psychologist, Subiaco

Chapter 13

Resolution for adult daughters

"It is important for adult daughters to resolve issues about their father"

CHAPTER TOPICS

- Why it is important for adult daughters to resolve issues about their fathers
- Steps that adult daughters can take to help resolve 'father issues' within themselves
- Steps to possible reconciliation with a father
- Is forgiveness possible?

Why it is important for adult daughters to resolve issues about their fathers

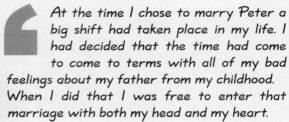

At the time I chose to marry Peter a big shift had taken place in my life. I had decided that the time had come to come to terms with all of my bad feelings about my father from my childhood. When I did that I was free to enter that marriage with both my head and my heart.

Yvonne deBlanc – social worker, Wembley

Father-daughter issues can surface after many years.[1,2] This has been called the 'sleeper effect' in some studies.[3] Anxiety in relationships, fear of intimacy and lack of trust are common outcomes.[4-6]

Many women, as they get older, develop insight into how their relationship with their father has actually affected them. It is often after they get married and have their own children that these issues become manifest, one way or another, as discussed in Chapter 1.

The most common issue that surfaces in women who reflect on their father-daughter relationship is a feeling that they missed out on the things that matter. For instance:

- dad didn't make them feel attractive, confident or worthy of respect
- he didn't ever really notice them
- he wasn't there for them
- they were not loved unconditionally by their fathers
- he never made them feel special or did any special things with them
- he abused their innocence and trust in him
- he did not protect them and they didn't feel safe with him

Feelings like that can hurt.

Many women have a clear view of how their relationship with their father has affected them

It is mostly when women begin to realise something was missing from their relationship with their dad that they begin think about it more deeply. Many women then seek to understand that relationship with their father, or lack of relationship, and try to understand themselves and their own reactions to their friends, partner, children and work colleagues.[7]

It is likely that women who read this book will reflect on their relationship with their father. Whilst in some cases this reflection might produce gratitude, in other cases it may lead to pain and grief. Old wounds might be opened as they sense even more deeply what sort of daughter-father relationship they could have had and what they may have missed out on. Women who have read the draft of this book have cried.

I was very nervous about writing a chapter about resolution and reconciliation for daughters – it is a sensitive area and it is easy to make things sound simpler than they really are. I am very nervous

Negative aspects of a woman's relationship with her father can affect her for the whole of her life

about passing on any advice at all in this area, even though it is not actually coming from me but from women who have tried these approaches and from experienced psychologists. I want to pass on what has worked for others. I feel that if I fail to acknowledge and address issues of resolution or reconciliation in a book like this and fail to pass on ideas from the women I interviewed, it would be unfair to the reader.

What I have chosen to do is to briefly discuss some issues relating to how daughters have dealt with issues of resolution or reconciliation between them and their fathers, acknowledging that this chapter can only stimulate your thinking on these issues. I have written this as a separate chapter specifically for women. Some readers may find it useful to pass it on to relevant men (e.g. their father) as a basis for discussion.

Why adult daughters should consider resolving issues about their fathers

- negative aspects of a woman's relationship with her father can affect her for the whole of her life
- this can lead to problems in relationships, especially marriage and parenting
- healing is possible and can lead to increased confidence
- reconciliation is also sometimes possible

I am guessing that other women (and men) could benefit from your own thoughts and ideas about any of your experiences of resolution or reconciliation, or lack of them, to broaden and strengthen our understanding of these issues.

I recommend strongly that if these things apply to you, that you seek extra input about such issues, preferably professional, because they can be difficult to talk about.

Gaining insight into a father-daughter relationship can help clarify a woman's current state of being

When I speak to women about their dads they tell me that the main reasons they wish to gain insight into their relationship with their dads is to understand why they are the way they are, why they act/react the way they do in their relationships with men and others, and to make sure that their children get what they themselves missed out on.

I noticed common themes in each story. The process of dealing with these problems is similar regardless of the nature of the problem.

Some, though not all, had achieved forgiveness and some healing and had moved into a closer, more understanding relationship with their dads and with their husbands.

This has sometimes surprised me, given the amount of pain some women have experienced. I was inspired by many of those conversations. I really hope that if you are in that situation, you will be able to get some resolution for yourself. I won't pretend it is easy.

I encourage you to take some of these steps. This chapter does not paint a full picture, so some relevant references and websites are listed on this book's website.

Some problems (e.g. sexual abuse), are harder to deal with, require professional help and don't often result in reconciliation with a father. These issues are discussed later in the chapter.

Steps to resolution

It can be hard to even begin to think about resolving issues about your father.

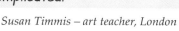

I'm not sure exactly what daughters need from their dads.

It's a very difficult thing for me to talk about because of my own relationship with my dad.

It is too complicated.

Susan Timmis – art teacher, London

The first step to resolution that was recommended by the women I interviewed was to be willing to examine yourself and not pretend that everything was perfect.

> Adult daughters can help themselves by firstly recognising their difficulties.
> It's not about blaming their fathers but just understanding the problem. That is half the battle.
> It's very important to try to resolve the issues within themselves first, rather than approach their fathers with anger.

Jean White – clinical psychologist, Melbourne

Many women benefit from trying to really understand how their father has affected them. Talking about things with others and trying to understand what your own reactions are to things that did or didn't happen can be best done with professional help if the hurt is great. Resolving things in yourself first, *independent* of your father, is a start.

This might involve forgiveness, though for many this is impossible. This is a forgiveness that does not depend upon his response.

Other components that have been useful for some women seeking resolution include recalling events and understanding your own story. Other things to consider include development of support systems, speaking out, individual and group psychotherapy, meditation, journalling, poetry, art, music, development of intimate relationships, forgiveness, loving yourself and others, evolving spirituality, development of voice and serving others.[8]

You need to accept that it is a hard road if the wounds are deep for you. You will probably get at least some resolution in yourself if you take these steps.

One reason that might encourage you to try to understand these things and not avoid them is that they will always be there. My interviewees have commented to me that the effects of problems in childhood are always there, lurking in the background and occasionally they take centre stage.

Think of it like the effect of gravity on birds - it is always operating but as long as they are flying they stay aloft. Gravity seems not to exist. But when they get tired gravity takes hold again and begins to drag them down. These childhood signals are always there and may get to you when you are feeling low. You need to be aware of this or you might get taken by surprise during tough times.

I will now let several women tell their stories of resolution and attempts at reconciliation.

I hope that the reader will be encouraged by these stories, especially if you have experienced similar feelings or actions. You might be inspired to write down your own story because stories can be 'good medicine'.[9]

> **These childhood signals are always there and may get to you when you are feeling low.**

There are no photos of these interviewees because they preferred to remain anonymous for the sakes of their families, and in some cases for the sake of their fathers who are still alive and with whom they are still working on reconciliation. The names have therefore been altered.

I have abbreviated their stories, but the full versions can be read on the book's website. You will have your own story too. You might consider writing to us to anonymously share your story via our website.

Judy's story – the distant father

My father

I had always been Dad's little girl. I adored my father. He was a builder and I used to go out with him in his truck when he was doing different jobs.

My mother died when I was nine years of age. She was 41 and had breast cancer which had spread throughout her body and he didn't handle the grief very well. So he went out a lot and did a lot of drinking. He was never home, but when he was home I was really happy. If I saw his car there in the driveway I would get really excited.

Abandonment

Looking back, I understand that it was his way of coping.

But after a year he sent me off to live with another family who had five other children. He sent me there because he couldn't cope and thought I would be better off with them. So I lost all of my family, not just my mother. I felt abandoned.

> "You can't be resentful and hold onto your resentments all the time. It's not good for you. You're the main one that gets hurt."

My self-destruction

By the time I was 16 I was going out and drinking a lot. Often I would go out drinking and just would not get home at all. Then there were weekends, lots of them, when I would just drink myself unconscious and spend most of the weekend that way. Alcohol gave me an escape and it felt good.

I was an alcoholic for many years but I didn't get into heroin until I met up with my daughter's father when I was 35.

For many years I blamed my family for my addictions, especially my dad. That's not the case now. I understand that I need to take responsibility for it, not blame others.

Resolution

It's hard to give advice to adult daughters of a father who has abandoned them or who has been distant from them in childhood. Dealing with that is especially hard if it seems like it will be impossible to resolve things with him.

First I would say "don't give up, keep trying".

But if it's not possible, you have to get on with life.

But in the end you have to forgive your father and acknowledge that maybe they thought they were doing the best for you at the time. You can't be resentful and hold onto your resentments all the time. It's not good for you. You're the main one that gets hurt. I did that for many years but I finally found that I could forgive my father.

Forgiveness

What brought me to that point of forgiveness? The first step happened when I stopped drinking and doing drugs because it gave me a clearer head and I was able to look at things more closely. Also I had counselling at the time which enabled me to deal with the issues that I had and helped me face reality. I used to blame lots of people but I don't do that now.

Brenda's story – physical and emotional abuse

My father

Dad was always short tempered and controlling. For example if he was going fishing he would insist that we go with him. But it wasn't relaxing, it was stressful. That's because he had such a temper that if we did anything wrong or we got bored and started to play around, he would yell at us. He had a strong temper and was very physical. He was not able to show love to any of his daughters.

Physical violence

I had lots of beltings as a child. I don't know how common they were - as a child you often imagine they were more common than they really were and that you were getting belted all of the time. But certainly I would lie on the bed and be hit with a belt. This would be for little things like being bossy to my sisters. My dad belted me up until the age of 11 or 12.

I have clear memories of my mother being hurt by my father. I slept in the next room and so I could hear her screaming and hear him hitting her. I cried. And I pulled a pillow over my head to try to stop myself from hearing it.

It's been a long journey.

Resolution

I was very much helped by counselling. That was the beginning of the start of the real healing that needs to be done in these kinds of situations. It helped me identify that the root cause of my controlling behaviour were things that happened in my childhood.

> "One of the important parts of that process is that I began to understand my father as a person as well as a father."

One of the important parts of that process is that I began to understand my father as a person as well as a father. That has meant that I don't just see things from the perspective of the 'hurt daughter'. That's true healing.

The first step a woman can take to heal a relationship with an abusive father is to get some insight into her feelings. But it's not just insight, it's more than that.

That first step in the pathway to forgiveness is to understand and know where the pain is greatest, and not to block it out.

It is important to not block out the memories. But then don't let that hurt linger otherwise it just interferes with other relationships.

> "That first step in the pathway to forgiveness is to understand and know where the pain is greatest, and not to block it out."

How do you stop the hurt lingering? I can't speak for others but for me it involved time talking with friends and having counselling. For me it also involved prayer.

Another thing that is critical in dealing with hurtful relationships with your father is to allow time for the healing.

Reconciliation

When I realised that I could begin to forgive my father, I knew that I had to start building up our relationship from scratch. So I decided to spend some time with him. Until then he hadn't engaged with me at all.

Now, when I look at my dad I don't see the man who was beating and raping his wife in the room next to mine, causing her to scream and causing me to cry and put my head under a pillow. I see a man who was a product of his own environment, who didn't know how to communicate, especially with women, who had a short temper, low self-esteem and a desperate need to be loved.

And I do love my dad now. I've learnt to love him. That love only began to happen once I began to understand why he is like he is.

My advice is 'don't expect to leap into this'. Take small steps. Don't expect to give or receive hugs if that makes the other person feel uncomfortable. An arm on the shoulder may be enough. Just take one step at a time.

I love my father now. I hug him and I talk to him.

You hear so many sad stories where women talk about their fathers as 'that bastard'. I am so grateful that I do not hold that resentment for my father because I have learnt forgiveness, understanding and love for him.

> "My advice is 'don't expect to leap into this'.
>
> Just take one step at a time."

There's nothing in my mind to forgive because I am at peace with what happened.

Hannah's story – sexual abuse

My father

My father fought in the Second World War (he was in the French Army) and he had actually expected to die during that war, so when he didn't he somehow lost his sense of direction. I don't know why.

Our family started to unravel after my sister died and Mum withdrew into herself. I imagine that during those years she withdrew from him sexually, but that is never an excuse for a man to abuse a child.

Sexual Abuse

My mother used to go out one night a week to choir practice and that was when my father began to abuse me. I don't know why he did it and there was an aspect of his personality which I think was a bit unhinged. But there was no excuse.

It was almost like my father courted me. He had a fascination with my hair. None of this was related to alcohol - he hardly ever drank.

I had felt very connected to my father and what he did destroyed that. It destroyed my sense of trust in him. Like other children in my situation I wanted the abuse to stop but I didn't want my special relationship to go.

The sexual abuse I experienced occurred at a very formative stage of my life. I did not have the words to express myself and to tell my father to stop. I was powerless and passive in it.

> "My specific advice to women who have been abused by their fathers is to get some help to start talking about it."

After my father abused me and our family disintegrated, I had a tough time from then on, particularly during my adolescence. I blamed myself because by telling my mother what my father was doing I had broken up the family. I was very depressed for a lot of that time.

Resolution

My specific advice to women who have been abused by their fathers is to get some help to start talking about it. It's very important that this secret comes out.

Therapy is a good way to come to terms with your own emotions and to develop the skills to talk to others about it. That's because it's a confidential relationship in which a person has the freedom to express herself knowing that the information won't be passed on to others. It's only because I have worked on this stuff in therapy that I am able to talk about it and have been able to work through it to this point in my life.

Forgiveness

Another piece of advice I would give to any woman who has been sexually abused is that forgiveness is very significant. I was able to forgive my father but not for a long time.

My ability to forgive happened slowly. One significant thing that I remember happening was reading a book called "What's

So Amazing About Grace" by Phillip Yancey. When I read that book I felt convicted about the need to forgive my father. and to forgive my two ex-husbands.

The reason that forgiveness is important is that when you fail to forgive someone. you end up being bound to them in some way. But forgiveness was a difficult road for me.

> "Therapy is a good way to come to terms with your own emotions and to develop the skills to talk to others about it."

Reconciliation

I acknowledge that in cases of abuse reconciliation is not usually possible for a variety of reasons and I certainly don't wish to suggest that it is. Mostly it is not, as in Hannah's story. But forgiveness has happened for others[10] and so has reconciliation.[11,12]

Having begun to resolve things within yourself, at least as much as you are able, you may choose to seek reconciliation with your father, or at least some understanding on his part and maybe an apology. That is a hard road.

Accept that you have some control over how you respond to knowledge about the father-daughter relationship but you have little control over how your father responds. In any case, he may have already died. If you believe that moving on depends upon your father you will almost certainly run into a roadblock. A dad who hurt you as a child ought not to be given too much opportunity to hurt or disappoint you again now that you are an adult.

> You have some control over how you respond to knowledge about the father-daughter relationship, but not how your father responds

You need to take control of your decisions about this. Don't let your father have that control. Don't let any response or lack of response from him define *you*.

One of the advantages of professional help over and above learning about your true feelings and responses, is the development of a 'vocabulary' to talk about your issues and a confidence to do so.

> Therapy is well worth it.
>
> It helps you resolve your own feelings about things. It also gives you the ability to communicate with other people about what happened, e.g. other members of your family such as your family of origin, your husband or whoever else.

Hannah

The main advice and common experience from women who have sought reconciliation with their fathers is that if they acted too quickly or abruptly it did not work, but produced a reaction from him. I can see why. Just because a daughter is gaining insight at a rapid rate does not mean her father is.

When to act

Don't wait until you feel love for your father or wait until you like him before you act. You may never love him, but you might want resolution. Sometimes it is best to take action thoughtfully without waiting for the right feelings.

Sometimes emotions *follow* actions rather than causing them. For example I remember reading about Corrie ten Boom, a Dutch lady whose family hid Jewish people during the Nazi occupation and for which they were imprisoned in a concentration camp. Her father and sister died during that internment.[13] After giving a lecture on the subject of the holocaust she was approached by a German man who explained that he had been an SS guard during the war.

He put out his hand to shake her hand but she could not respond. She was paralysed by hatred. She did not want to shake his hand.

But she finally did so simply because she felt she should. Then a remarkable thing happened – she felt love and forgiveness for him *as* she was holding his hand. The emotion came after she had acted out of obligation, not *before*.

> Don't wait until you *feel* love for your father, or even like him, before you choose to act

Consider doing something yourself to act into the situation, even if you are seething with righteous indignation.

These things can be naturally very hard for you to deal with and they also may be hard for your dad to deal with. He is not likely to be free of the very problem that he had that caused him to behave the way he did. If he had an awful dad himself, you won't be able to fix that for him. If he had major psychological problems himself, he probably won't be free of them now.

What if dad isn't interested?

If dad does not respond don't be surprised because fairy-tale outcomes are not common. If he does respond at all, especially if he does so warmly and openly, you might see it as icing on the cake, not the whole cake. You can only control and 'own' your part of the reconciliation. But that is simply an input, not an output. It will help you but you can't control the outcome so try not to stew about it.

In fact your actions should probably not really be aimed at eliciting a response from him but to reflect your character and what *you* choose to do.

Give up if necessary. Don't spend the rest of your life seeking a response from him - the fundamental self-centredness that caused him to hurt you in the first place will probably still be there.

It is most likely that he hasn't come very far, certainly not as far you might hope and even imagine.

Early steps

Be gentle with your father. Your gentleness with your father will be a further reflection of your character, rather than what he deserves. It may help achieve some measure of reconciliation.

> Be gentle with your father and allow lots of time

> I began having him around to visit our home. And I began to talk to him. I'd ask him about what he was doing, what he was enjoying and what he thought about things. Of course he wouldn't ask me about my life. But I don't wait for that and I don't resent it if he doesn't do it. So I'm enjoying talking with him even though I am the one doing the asking.
>
> Children are a good vehicle for this healing too.
>
> *Brenda*

When you choose words, choose non-accusatory ones if you want a .result rather than just the chance to offload all your anger on to him.

Find something good to say about him, about what you appreciate about him. It might not be anything about your childhood but about his role as a grandfather, his work, the way he looked after your mother or something else. And don't follow this with a 'but…..'. When an affirmation is followed by a statement starting with 'but….' it often destroys that affirmation in the listener's heart ('I was being buttered up for a but…').

Whether you can say 'I love you' is a harder issue, but if you can, do so, without expecting anything much in return.

Reconciliation took a long time but I do love my dad now. I've learnt to love him. Eventually I decided I wanted to tell him.

We were taking the children on holidays and invited my father to come and stay with us - we thought he would enjoy it there too. So one afternoon I went for a walk with my father. I was very nervous. I had that silly butterfly feeling inside. I didn't know when I should tell him. Do I say it now? Or do I wait? Do I say it now? Finally we stopped on a cliff and looked out over the ocean and I just put my hand on his shoulder and said 'Dad, I love you.'

What did he do? He smiled and put his hand around my shoulder.

What's interesting is that because he had physically abused me as a child and because I hated him, I couldn't handle him hugging or kissing me. But I find that I can now handle him hugging and kissing me since I have learnt to love him again.

Barbara – teacher, Brisbane

I did a personal development course once and the issue of 'expressing love' came up. My dad had never told me he loved me but I hadn't said it either. I realised that it was up to me, not him, to make the first move. So I decided to tell him I loved him.

I went to his house. He was outside in his yard watering his garden.

I was really nervous.

I didn't say it smoothly, and bumbled on a bit about the course I was doing, but I did manage to tell him that I loved him. He stopped and said to me that he loved me too and we hugged and I cried.

When I drove to my course the next day I cried nearly all the way there.

Renata – actor, New Jersey

He may apologise for what he did but he probably will not, so don't wait for it or hang out for it.

Having tried some of these strategies, what do you do next? It is impossible to know because every situation is different. There are things that women I spoke to have found helpful. One way to begin is to show an interest in your father's own past, whether he is alive or dead. Understanding a father's background has been shown to be helpful.[14] You might try to find out more about his life, particularly his childhood, the difficulties he experienced and what his family was like.

> It's been a very difficult thing for me to talk about my father - it's too painful. I loved him but loathed him.
> I found out that Dad had polio as a sixteen year old and was paralysed. He spent two years in an iron lung in hospital. His mother had never once gone to see him at all during those two years. She was not a warm loving mother and my father suffered because of that.

Sarah Thomas – teacher, Glasgow

The next step is to write down your thoughts and memories, your appreciations and regrets. Many women have written letters to their fathers and found that to be helpful and less confronting, especially if it is affirming.

If your father has died it becomes harder. You can write what you might have liked to say to him if he were still alive. Some women then place that note near his grave, others throw it into the sea, others read it then burn it. There are probably other things that are similarly helpful. Maybe keep a spare copy and share it with someone who loves you, perhaps your husband.

> My father was dead already before the issue of forgiveness came up. It took a long time.
> How do you forgive someone who is dead?

Amanda

Forgiveness

Forgiveness might be important for *you*, rather than as a means of reconciliation.

> The reason that forgiveness is important is that when you fail to forgive someone, you end up being bound to them in some way. This is because you are always holding them to account. That means that whenever they're with you they always feel defensive and they feel an urge to rationalise their behaviour. But when you forgive someone, not only do you get your own sense of freedom and liberation but you release them.
> They then become free to think about their role and to deal with their own consciences.

Maureen – computer programmer, San Diego

> Forgiveness was a difficult road for me. But I have forgiven my father. There's no residual hate or anger left in me.
> The only thing I still have is a sense of sadness about the loss of relationship with my father. But there's nothing left that I need to forgive.

Helen

Resolution and reconciliation
– some things to think about

Fathers and father-figures

- be absolutely safe and trustworthy with girls you interact with
- encourage other father-figures to be the same
- if you have problems in this area you must seek professional help
- always be willing to listen and apologise to your daughter

Adult daughters

- be willing to consider the issues raised in this chapter about father-daughter relationships and how that might still be affecting you
- don't be afraid to seek professional help via your family doctor, counsellor or psychologist
- if other women share with you their struggles, sadness or even abuse, listen with an open mind – most girls/women who have suffered as children are not believed at first

Husbands

- be willing to help and support your wife as she deals with issues between herself and her father
- be patient, especially if you feel uncomfortable listening to it all
- try to understand
- don't jump in and judge or 'solve' the problems
- don't trivialise her concerns
- forgiveness is hard so don't expect too much of your wife too quickly
- walk with your wife on this journey

Postcript

I will conclude where I began, with a dream that every girl will have a strong father and/or father-figure in her life, one who makes her feel beautiful, worthwhile, capable and special.

I dream that all girls will have a father and/or father-figure who listens to them with kindness and unconditional acceptance and love, and who makes an effort to create special times with her.

I also dream that every adult daughter will gain insight and inner strength by better understanding her relationship with her father, whether it was good or bad.

I dream too that all husbands/partners will seek to understand more about the women they love, especially the things that make them the way they are. And I hope that these men are patient and understanding in the process.

I dream that *every* man, young or old, who interacts with girls will not neglect them but will make an effort to make them feel special, attractive and capable.

Our communities would be happier and healthier if that dream came true.

References and additional material

There are over 300 references in the book so for space reasons these have been listed on the book's website, along with recommended books.

www.brucerobinson.com.au / daughters / references

Additional material for each chapter:

1. **The father-daughter relationship**
www.brucerobinson.com.au / daughters / relationship

2. **Father-figures**
www.brucerobinson.com.au / daughters / father-figures

3. **Beauty**
www.brucerobinson.com.au / daughters / beauty

4. **Confidence**
www.brucerobinson.com.au / daughters / confidence

5. **Drugs**
www.brucerobinson.com.au / daughters / drugs

6. **Learning**
www.brucerobinson.com.au / daughters / learning

7. **Men**
www.brucerobinson.com.au / daughters / men

8. **Unconditional love**
www.brucerobinson.com.au / daughters / love

9. **Listening**
www.brucerobinson.com.au / daughters / listening

10. **Specialness**
www.brucerobinson.com.au / daughters / specialness

11. **Dad dates and trips**
www.brucerobinson.com.au / daughters / datesandtrips

12. **Overcoming blocks**
www.brucerobinson.com.au / daughters / blocks

13. **Resolution**
www.brucerobinson.com.au / daughters / resolution